TRUE GRITS

Also by Lee Pfeiffer

The Clint Eastwood Scrapbook
The Films of Clint Eastwood (with Boris Zmijewsky)
The Films of Harrison Ford (with Michael Lewis)
The Films of Sean Connery (with Phil Lisa)
The Films of Tom Hanks (with Michael Lewis)
The Official Andy Griffith Show Scrapbook
The Incredible World of 007 (with Philip Lisa)
The John Wayne Scrapbook
The Ultimate Clint Eastwood Trivia Book (with Michael Lewis)
The Essential 007 (with Dave Worrall)

Also by Michael Lewis

The Cheapskate's Guide to Walt Disney World (with Debbi Lacey)
The Films of Harrison Ford (with Lee Pfeiffer)
The Films of Tom Hanks (with Lee Pfeiffer)
The Ultimate Clint Eastwood Trivia Book (with Lee Pfeiffer)
The Ultimate James Bond Trivia Book

TRUE GRITS

RECIPES INSPIRED BY THE MOVIES OF

JOHN WAYNE

Written and compiled by
Lee Pfeiffer and Michael Lewis

A BIRCH LANE PRESS BOOK
Published by Carol Publishing Group

A Birch Lane Press Book
Published by Carol Publishing Group
Birch Lane Press is a registered trademark of Carol Communications, Inc.

Editorial, sales and distribution, and rights and permissions inquiries should be
addressed to Carol Publishing Group, 120 Enterprise Avenue, Secaucus, N.J. 07094.

In Canada: Canadian Manda Group, One Atlantic Avenue, Suite 105, Toronto,
Ontario M6K 3E7

Carol Publishing Group books may be purchased in bulk at special discounts for
sales promotion, fund-raising, or educational purposes. Special editions can be
created to specifications. For details, contact Special Sales Department, Carol
Publishing Group, 120 Enterprise Avenue, Secaucus, N.J. 07094.

Manufactured in the United States of America
10 9 8 7 6 5 4 3 2 1

Library of Congress Cataloging-in-Publication Data

Pfeiffer, Lee.
    True grits : recipes inspired by the movies of John Wayne / written and
compiled by Lee Pfeiffer and Michael Lewis.
        p.   cm.
    "Birch Lane Press book."
    Includes index.
    ISBN 1-55972-454-4 (sc)
    1. Cookery.   2. Motion pictures—Miscellanea.   3. Wayne, John,
1907-1979—Miscellanea.   I. Lewis, Michael (Michael D.), 1962–.
II. Title.
TX714.P467   1998
641.5—dc21   98–4627
                                                                      CIP

To grandma Sophie Thumann, who first taught me the delicious joys of a home-cooked meal
—Michael Lewis

CONTENTS

"Awright, which one of you varmints dreamed up 'Rooster Heartburn'?"

ACKNOWLEDGMENTS

Individually thanking every contributor in this space would be tantamount to crediting every Mexican soldier in *The Alamo*. Suffice it to say that we are most grateful for the enthusiastic cooperation of the friends, relatives, and other people who should know better, for providing such a wide range of recipes. Many of the braver souls, unafraid of being linked to our "inspired" titles based on the Duke's films, have allowed us to specifically credit individual recipes with their names. (Would *you* want to take credit for The Flan Who Shot Liberty Valance?) We especially thank Amy Lewis, Jim and Judy Hamilton, and Kathy and Paul Swindells: the results of the free dinner contest are forthcoming.

A few nonrecipe contributors deserve high praise for coming up with some of the most notorious "titles so bad, they're good." Thus, we acknowledge Janet and Nicole Pfeiffer as well as good friend Zachary Christ. (As the latter two cowpokes are eleven and twelve years old, respectively, this proves that bad taste is not a monopoly enjoyed by adults.)

At Carol Publishing, thanks to our long-suffering friends Steven Schragis, Bruce Bender, Gary Fitzgerald, Bill Wolfsthal, Andrea Cuperman, Meryl Earl, Donald Davidson, Allan J. Wilson, Greg Wilkin, and all the rest too numerous to mention. Bet you guys didn't really think we could pull off a cookbook, did you?

Most of all, thanks to the legions of fellow Wayne aficionados worldwide who continue to keep the Duke's legacy thriving.

"Can someone please pass The Greatest Jell-O Ever Mold?"

WITHOUT RESERVATIONS

We'll state the embarrassing truth up front: our idea of gourmet dining is a twenty-pack served at midnight at the White Castle in Jersey City, New Jersey. As we recognize our limitations in the kitchen, we are prudent enough to insure the readers' health by having people with considerably more culinary skill provide the recipes herein. However, let's face another fact: this volume is less a guidebook to improving one's cooking talents than it is an homage to our favorite movie star. The only thing more enjoyable than watching John Wayne films for the umpteenth time is to get paid to write about them. With countless books already dedicated to serious examination of the Duke's career, we thought it was time for a different approach. As celebrity-inspired cookbooks are all the rage, why not honor America's most popular actor of all time with recipes based on his most notable films? (Especially when such a work has a built-in, unspeakably catchy-yet-awful title like *True Grits!*)

While the recipes have admittedly been chosen on the basis of how they lend themselves to spoofing Wayne film titles, each actually works and is a tried-and-true delight. One thing is certain: this must be the most eclectic dossier of information and recipes ever compiled. Where else can you find instructions on how to prepare everything from Chinese food to Jell-O molds, all accompanied by photos and trivia from John Wayne's films and jokey recipe titles cornier than the script for *The Conqueror?* If How the Wurst Was Done doesn't make you flinch, then In Ham's Way should do the job! Still, we hope readers won't be snobby and refuse to give these tasty dishes a try. As Wayne cautioned the prudish Colonel Travis in *The Alamo:* "Step down off your high horse, mister. You don't get lard less'n you boil the hog!" We still don't have the faintest idea what that means, but it always *sounded* good. Besides, if you look hard enough in the pages that follow, you just may find an appropriate recipe which will allow you to take the Duke's advice literally and boil a hog.

We won't waste any more time trying to convince readers that these recipes have true value. Chances are that if you're reading this book it's probably not because you are a French chef, but more likely a dyed-in-the-wool Duke Wayne fan who must add this to your collection. In any event, *True Grits* is far more practical as a collectible than one of those velvet paintings of Duke Wayne meeting Elvis in heaven. Besides, regardless of your taste in food, the scattergun approach to the recipes herein virtually guarantees something for everyone. (We admit, though, that we probably cater to folks like us, who firmly believe that the best dining establishments are those which inevitably have eighteen-wheeler trucks parked in front of them. We try to cater to the simple needs of the "meat-and-potatoes" crowd.)

So what're you waitin' for, Pilgrim? Stop burnin' daylight and start cookin'!

Lee Pfeiffer and Michael Lewis

Important Note: We've tried to give you a basic idea of what equipment you'll need to prepare each dish, but to make sure you're fully prepared, read the recipe first before you dive right into it so you'll get a basic idea of what size mixing bowls you'll need, and so forth.

SUNRISE BREAKFASTS

JOHN WAYNE · GLEN CAMPBELL · KIM DARBY

DANS UN FILM DE
HAL WALLIS

100 DOLLARS POUR UN SHERIF

TRUE GRIT

100 DOLLARS VOOR EEN SHERIF

avec
JEREMY SLATE · ROBERT DUVALL · STROTHER MARTIN

REGIE
HENRY HATHAWAY

SCENARIO
MARGUERITE ROBERTS

D'APRÈS LE ROMAN DE
CHARLES PORTIS

Title Song Sung by GLEN CAMPBELL · Music Scored by ELMER BERNSTEIN

TECHNICOLOR®

True Grit

Cast: John Wayne, Glen Campbell, Kim Darby, Jeremy Slate,
Robert Duvall, Alfred Ryder, Strother Martin, Jeff Corey
Director: Henry Hathaway
Released by Paramount Pictures (1969)

When John Wayne strode to the podium to accept his Oscar in 1970, he quipped, "Wow! If I'd have known that, I'd have put that patch on thirty-five years earlier!" The remark was in reference to his now immortal portrayal of Marshal Rooster Cogburn, the "one-eyed fat man" of *True Grit,* the 1969 western directed by Duke's old crony Henry Hathaway. Wayne wanted to play the role from the minute he read Charles Portis's novel in galley form, but found that producer Hal Wallis had secured the rights first. Prophetically, Wallis agreed that Duke was the only actor who could bring Rooster to life on the big screen.

True Grit marked a renaissance for John Wayne. While his films had remained popular with the public, critics had all but given up on the possibility of Wayne "stretching" as an actor beyond a very limited screen persona. With the role of Rooster Cogburn, Wayne proved that with the right director and screenplay, he had the ability to reinvigorate the acting ability he had shown in his earlier work with John Ford and Howard Hawks. Even critics in such traditionally Wayne-hostile territory as New York were enamored with his work in *Grit,* as evidenced by *New York Daily News* film reviewer Kathleen Carroll calling the film "John

Wayne's finest moment." On Oscar night the Academy agreed and awarded the Duke the Best Actor trophy, despite such stiff competition as Dustin Hoffman, Jon Voight, Peter O'Toole, and Richard Burton.

Did You Know . . . ?

★ The Duke had only been nominated for an Oscar once before: for the 1949 war epic *Sands of Iwo Jima* (though when interviewed he would routinely—and erroneously—insist that he was also nominated for *She Wore a Yellow Ribbon,* which was released the same year).

★ Glen Campbell's theme song for *True Grit* was also nominated for an Oscar. (It lost to B. J. Thomas's "Raindrops Keep Fallin' on My Head," from *Butch Cassidy and the Sundance Kid.*)

True Grits

Mattie made this simple dish for Mr. Cogburn, a marshal of simple needs and hard-bitten determination, while they were out tracking Chaney.

INGREDIENTS:
  1 *cup medium ground grits*
1½ *cups water*
  ⅓ *teaspoon salt*

EQUIPMENT:
Medium saucepan with lid

Put the salt in the water. Bring water to a boil. Stir in the grits slowly and bring to a second boil. Simmer, covered, for 20 minutes, stirring occasionally. Serve hot.

If, unlike Rooster, you like more flavorful grits, add salt, pepper, butter, and milk to taste. Your favorite grated cheese also adds a special flavor.

True Grits: They're not just for breakfast!

They Were Expendable

Cast: Robert Montgomery, John Wayne, Donna Reed, Jack Holt,
    Ward Bond, Marshall Thompson
Director: John Ford
Released by MGM (1945)

The supreme patriot, director John Ford had gained praise during World War II with stunning documentaries such as *The Battle of Midway*, which were commissioned by the U.S. government. Back in Hollywood, Ford began a film adaptation of *They Were Expendable,* a bestselling book about Lt. John Bulkeley, who developed the lightly armed PT boats into major offensive weapons for the U.S. Navy in the dark days following the attack on Pearl Harbor. Bulkeley was portrayed on-screen by Robert Montgomery, who traded his status as a Hollywood leading man for that of the real-life war hero and PT boat commander. John Wayne was cast in the supporting—but pivotal—role of his second in command, a hot-tempered and impatient junior officer whose eagerness to strike back at the Japanese often undermines his sense of prudent strategy.

The film featured some of the most realistic action sequences ever shot. Ford succeeded in his goal of presenting the war in a believable and frightening way. By all accounts, the atmosphere on the set was grim, probably because the Pearl Harbor disaster was still so fresh in everyone's mind. Ford anticipated the film would be released while the war still raged, but the dropping of the atomic bomb brought the conflict to a conclusion while *Expendable* was still being filmed. When it finally premiered, it was enthusiastically received by critics, but largely ignored by a jubilant public, which sought lighter-hearted cinematic fare. Still, the film remains a major achievement in the careers of John Ford and Duke Wayne.

Did You Know . . . ?

★ The screenplay for *They Were Expendable* was written by World War I flying ace Frank "Spig" Wead, whom Wayne would later portray in *The Wings of Eagles* (1957).

They Were Eggspendable

A zesty scrambled egg dish to start your day.

INGREDIENTS:
- 4 *large eggs*
- 1 *teaspoon chili powder*
- 1 *tablespoon mild salsa*
- 1 *cup mild picante sauce*
- 1 *cup shredded Cheddar cheese*

4 *slices bacon*

EQUIPMENT:
Medium bowl
Medium frying pan or saucepan

Fry the bacon until browned and drain. Beat the eggs in the bowl; mix in the chili powder, salsa, bacon (broken into pieces), and cheese. Melt a pat of butter in the frying pan and spread it around, then pour in the egg mixture. Scramble everything together over medium heat until well cooked (slightly browned). Top with picante sauce. Serves 4.

Girls Demand Eggs Omelet

(Girls Demand Excitement, 1931)

The girls at school know what they want, and they want this tasty omelet.

INGREDIENTS:
- 1 medium tomato
- 1 small green pepper
- ½ onion
- 2 sprigs parsley
- 1 stalk celery
- Handful olives
- Handful mushrooms
- Dash chili powder (optional)

4 large eggs
Salt and pepper to taste

EQUIPMENT:
Medium bowl
Small saucepan
Medium omelet pan or frying pan

Peel the tomato, place in the bowl with the pepper, onion, parsley, celery, olives, and mushrooms, and chop all together. Place in the saucepan, add the seasonings and cook over a low flame 2 to 3 minutes. Beat the eggs, then pour into the omelet pan or buttered frying pan on low heat. As soon as the eggs begins to cook, add the vegetable mixture. Cook until very lightly browned, about 8 minutes. Serves 2 to 4.

Brannigan

Cast: John Wayne, Richard Attenborough, Judy Geeson, Mel Ferrer,
John Vernon
Director: Douglas Hickox
Released by United Artists (1975)

The Duke's in London . . . God Save the Queen!" read the tag line on the ads for *Brannigan*. Following his success as *McQ*, Wayne opted to stay in contemporary surroundings for another police thriller, albeit a much more humorous one. *Brannigan* is to Wayne what *Coogan's Bluff* (1968) was to Clint Eastwood; both actors portrayed tough cops as "fish out of water" in hostile surroundings. In Wayne's case, he is sent to London to extradite a criminal. Predictably, he clashes with the local stuffed-shirt police, headed by Richard Attenborough. While somewhat clichéd, *Brannigan* makes imaginative use of its London locales, and Wayne looks delighted to be in a change of environment. Although well into his sixties, he proves he can still hold his own in barroom brawls and action sequences.

The oddball casting of Wayne opposite Attenborough works quite well, as the two adversaries they portray gradually build mutual respect for each other. John Vernon, the preeminent villain in seemingly every film shot in the 1970s, is a bit of a bore, but Mel Ferrer is believably sinister as his accomplice.

Brannigan marked Wayne's final cinematic foray into the contemporary world. For his last two films—*Rooster Cogburn* (1975) and *The Shootist* (1976)—he would return once more to the western genre, which made him a star.

Did You Know . . . ?

★ The original title for *Brannigan* was "Joe Battle."

Bran Again Muffins

The great detective often started his day with these delicious muffins.

INGREDIENTS:
- 3 cups bran flakes
- 1 cup boiling water
- 1 stick oleo
- 1½ cups sugar
- 2 large eggs
- 2 cups buttermilk
- 2½ cups all-purpose flour
- 2 teaspoons baking soda
- 1 teaspoon salt

EQUIPMENT:
Medium bowl
Large bowl
Sifter
Muffin tins

In a medium bowl, pour water over one cup of bran and let stand while mixing the rest of the batter. Beat the eggs; add sugar and buttermilk and the rest of the bran flakes and oleo. Sift the flour, soda, and salt, and then add to the egg mixture. Add the bran, which had been mixed with the hot water. Mix well. Bake for 20 minutes at 400° F. in greased muffin tins. Makes 30 muffins.

Hondo takes aim at a hearty breakfast.

Hondo

Cast: John Wayne, Geraldine Page, Ward Bond, Michael Pate,
    James Arness, Rodolfo Acosta, Lee Aaker
Director: John Farrow
Released by Warner Bros (1953)

By 1953, John Wayne had become one of the few stars to successfully form his own production company. He and his partner Bob Fellows purchased the rights to a Louis L'Amour short story titled "Hondo," which centered on a mysterious gunman's attempt to rescue a widow and her young son in hostile Indian territory—and falling in love with her in the process.

Shooting *Hondo* was an unpleasant experience for Wayne. He was in the middle of a messy and sensationalized divorce from his wife Chata; he was coping with budget concerns on the remote set in Mexico; and he found himself short-tempered with his costar Geraldine Page, whose training on Broadway did not complement Wayne's acting style.

Hondo was originally shot in 3-D, but when the process proved to be costly and unpopular with theater owners, it was released in a standard 35mm version. The film became a sizable hit, although director John Farrow's skills fell somewhat short of the style that "Pappy" John Ford would have inevitably brought to the project. Despite its success,

Hondo had the misfortune of being released in the same year as the similarly-themed *Shane,* starring Alan Ladd, which won the lion's share of critical raves and audience enthusiasm.

Hondo, one of a handful of films whose rights are controlled by the Wayne family, was out of distribution for many years. In the early 1990s it was finally released on video to highly profitable results.

Did You Know . . . ?

★ The only time *Hondo* has been seen in 3-D was in its initial week of national release in theaters and in a TV broadcast in the late 1980s. (Viewers could pick up special *Hondo* 3-D glasses at 7–11 convenience stores for the broadcast.)

Hondocakes

Pancakes that taste better than the rest because they're in 3-D!

INGREDIENTS:
2 large eggs
2 tablespoons sugar
1 teaspoon salt
2½ cups buttermilk
2 cups all-purpose flour
1 teaspoon baking powder
1 teaspoon baking soda

¼ cup hot water
2 tablespoons salted butter
or margarine

EQUIPMENT:
Large mixing bowl
Griddle or large frying pan

Beat the eggs, melt the butter, and set each aside. In the bowl, combine the eggs, sugar, salt, and buttermilk. Sift the flour and baking powder together, then blend in the egg mixture. Add the melted butter. Fry on a hot, greased griddle over low heat until both sides are golden brown, approximately five minutes. Serve with a pat of butter and syrup to taste. Yields about 20 hotcakes.

MOVE 'EM OUT
APPETIZERS

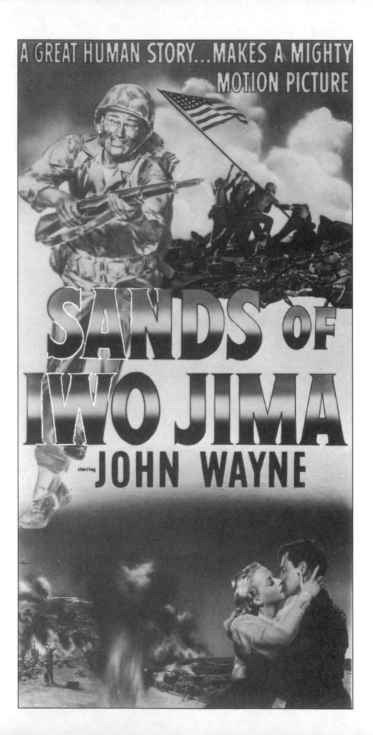

Sands of Iwo Jima

Cast: John Wayne, John Agar, Adele Mara, Forrest Tucker,
Wally Cassell, James Brown
Director: Allan Dwan
Released by Republic Pictures (1949)

John Wayne had been nominated for an Academy Award only twice in his career. He won the Oscar for his performance in *True Grit* (1969), but had been nominated twenty years previously for *Sands of Iwo Jima* (though Duke occasionally—and incorrectly—insisted he had been nominated for *She Wore a Yellow Ribbon,* also released in 1949). *Sands of Iwo Jima* cast Wayne as tough-as-nails Marine sergeant Stryker, who berates and works his men ceaselessly, inevitably incurring their wrath. They realize, however, that Stryker has succeeded in making them a crack fighting unit, an attribute which comes in handy during the bloody assault on the island of Iwo Jima.

The role of Stryker was a pivotal one for the Duke. Just as Wayne had become the leading symbol of the cowboy hero, *Sands of Iwo Jima* established him as the quintessential twentieth-century U.S. soldier. Under Allan Dwan's capable direction, the film succeeds in debunking the myth that war is glorious. *Sands* presents the battlefield as a no-man's land in which death can come unexpectedly at any second.

Indeed, it does for Wayne's character in the memorable and touching finale.

The movie was a significant hit at the box office, and Wayne's Oscar nomination was Hollywood's official recognition that he was an important and respected leading man.

Did You Know . . . ?

★ Kirk Douglas was originally envisioned by director Allan Dwan to play the role of Sgt. Stryker.

Sandwiches of Iwo Jima

Shrimp toast—a great appetizer to serve at your party to celebrate a flag raising.

INGREDIENTS:
- *½ pound large raw shrimp (cleaned, shelled, and deveined)*
- *4 water chestnuts*
- *1 teaspoon salt*
- *1 teaspoon sugar*
- *1 tablespoon corn starch*
- *1 large egg*
- *6 slices of bread (white or wheat), at least 2 days old*
- *2 cups cooking oil (we prefer canola)*

EQUIPMENT:
Medium bowl
Medium frying pan
Frying thermometer

In the medium bowl lightly beat the egg and add the salt, sugar, and corn starch; beat together until smooth. Chop the water chestnuts, and mince the shrimp. Mix together with egg batter. Trim the crusts off the bread and cut each slice into four triangles. Spread each triangle with 1 teaspoon of the shrimp mixture.

Heat oil in the pan to 375° F. on frying thermometer. Lower the bread into the oil, shrimp-side down. After 1 minute, turn over and fry until golden. Serves 4 to 6.

The Telegraph Ale Meatballs

(*The Telegraph Trail,* 1933)

The chuck wagon on the supply train always had a hot plate of these cocktail meatballs at the ready.

INGREDIENTS:
 2 slices white bread
 1 12-ounce can or bottle beer
 1 pound lean ground beef
 ½ cup shredded part-skim
      mozzarella
 ¼ teaspoon salt
      Dash pepper
 3 tablespoons salted butter
 ½ cup chopped fresh onion
 2 tablespoons dark brown sugar

 2 tablespoons white vinegar
 2 tablespoons beef stock
 1 tablespoon all-purpose
      flour

EQUIPMENT:
Medium bowl
Cookie sheet
Large saucepan
Paper towels
Toothpicks

Cut the bread into one-inch cubes and soak in a half cup of beer. Combine the beef with the cheese, salt, pepper, and soaked bread. Mix well and form into small meatballs. Arrange in a single layer on a cookie sheet. Bake for 15 minutes at 350° F.

While the meatballs are cooking, saute the onions in the butter until tender. Stir in the sugar, vinegar, beef stock, and the remaining beer. Thicken with the flour. Simmer about 10 minutes.

Drain the cooked meatballs well on paper towels. Add to the sauce and simmer 20 minutes. Serve with toothpicks.

The Horse Soldiers

Cast: John Wayne, William Holden, Constance Towers,
Althea Gibson, Hoot Gibson, Anna Lee, Russell Simpson
Director: John Ford
Released by United Artists (1959)

The Horse Soldiers had all the ingredients of a major box office hit: the surefire teaming of John Wayne and John Ford, along with the powerhouse presence of William Holden. For various reasons, however, this richly entertaining film failed to ignite sparks with audiences despite some of the most memorable sequences to be found in any Ford production. To be sure, the famed director was by all accounts rather grumpy and disinterested during filming. His mood worsened after he blamed himself for the death of a stuntman during an action sequence. By his own admission, Ford was on virtual "automatic pilot," counting the minutes until the movie was completed.

Still, *The Horse Soldiers* boasts a terrific screenplay in which Wayne leads a daring raid behind Confederate lines to inflict maximum damage to railroads. His character is in constant conflict with a cynical doctor played by Holden, one of the few actors whose screen presence was big enough to stand up to the Duke's. The film features some superbly staged action sequences and the usual sterling supporting performances from the Ford stock company. Despite the anemic box office reception accorded the film, it remains an effort which stands tall in the canon of Wayne-Ford collaborations.

Did You Know . . . ?

★ Althea Gibson, who played the slave girl Lukey, had already achieved fame as an Olympic tennis star.

The Hors D'oeuvres Soldiers

If these cocktail franks were served to "Pappy" during the production of the film, it might have cheered him.

INGREDIENTS:
- 1 *cup tomato puree*
- 3 *tablespoons cider vinegar*
- ⅓ *cup firmly packed light brown sugar*
- 1½ *teaspoons chili powder*
- 1 *garlic clove*
- 2 *5½-ounce packages cocktail franks*

EQUIPMENT:
Medium saucepan
Chafing dish
Toothpicks

Mix all the ingredients except the franks in the saucepan and simmer uncovered, stirring occasionally. Add the franks and simmer uncovered for about 10 minutes or until hot, stirring occasionally. Pour into a chafing dish and serve with toothpicks.

The Hot Wings of Eagles

(*The Wings of Eagles*, 1957)

This squadron of chicken wings is a tasty treat. Let them fly over your next get-together! Thanks to "Commander" Kathy Swindells for this recipe.

INGREDIENTS:
1 *large package of chicken wings (20 or more)*
1½ *cups Red Hot sauce*
1 *stick salted butter*
2 *tablespoons orange juice*
1 *fresh jalapeño pepper*

EQUIPMENT:
Small pot
Casserole dish

Bake wings at 350° F. until thoroughly cooked—45 minutes to an hour. Finely chop the jalapeno and set it aside. Melt the butter, stir in the hot sauce and peppers, then pour over the wings while they are still hot. Let the chicken simmer in a still-warm, turned-off oven, for about 10 minutes. Serve with blue cheese dressing and celery stalks, if you like.

Cahill's United States Mushrooms

(*Cahill, United States Marshal,* 1973)

Appetizing fungi sure to satisfy any marshal or deputy. Thanks to "Deputy" Paul Swindells for this recipe.

INGREDIENTS:
- 1 *large (16-ounce) package of fresh, white button mushrooms*
- 1 *10-ounce box frozen spinach*
- ½ *pound ham*
- ¾ *stick salted butter*
- 3 *garlic cloves*
- ⅓ *cup Italian flavored bread crumbs*
- ¼ *cup Parmesan cheese*
- 2 *teaspoons ground nutmeg*
  Salt and pepper to taste

EQUIPMENT:
Cutting board
1-quart glass casserole dish
Large frying pan

Shred the ham, then crush the garlic, and set aside. Separate the mushroom caps from the stems, then take 7 or 8 stems, dice finely, and set aside. In a large frying pan, add 1 tablespoon of butter and saute the ham in the melted butter. Then add the spinach and diced mushroom stems. Saute over medium heat for about 15 minutes, then add the garlic, bread crumbs, Parmesan cheese, salt, and pepper. Let simmer about 10 more minutes.

Now, take the mushroom caps and, with a teaspoon, fill with the stuffing. Place the mushrooms in a glass casserole dish. Melt the remaining butter in the pan, pour over the mushrooms, and bake at 350° F. for 15 to 20 minutes, or until the mushrooms turn golden brown. Remove from the oven and sprinkle with nutmeg.

The Comancheros

Cast: John Wayne, Stuart Whitman, Ina Balin, Nehemiah Persoff,
Lee Marvin, Michael Ansara, Patrick Wayne, Bruce Cabot
Director: Michael Curtiz
Released by Twentieth Century–Fox (1961)

By the late 1950s, John Wayne had discovered—much to his horror—that his finance manager had squandered his hard-won fortune in a series of bad investments. Coupled with losses incurred from *The Alamo,* the Duke found himself deep in debt at an age when many people look forward to retirement. Not one for self-pity, the Duke began making films at a record pace. His 1961 western *The Comancheros* was a bright spot for the actor. It boasted a witty and exciting screenplay and provided him with another opportunity to work with many of his old cronies.

The Comancheros features Wayne as a Texas ranger who coerces a charming con man (Stuart Whitman) into accompanying him into Indian territory to infiltrate and destroy a gun-running operation. The film provided some wonderful action sequences, and the chemistry between Wayne and his fellow cast members seemed genuine. There are a number of good supporting performances, primarily from Lee Marvin and Nehemiah Persoff, and Elmer Bernstein's thundering score proved to be quite memorable.

For the Duke, a film as enjoyable to make as this helped distract him from the realization that he had a long road ahead of him if he were to regain financial security.

Did You Know . . . ?

★ The director of *The Comancheros,* the legendary Michael Curtiz, was so ill during filming that John Wayne quietly directed much of the film. Curtiz died a few months after the movie's premiere.

The Clamancheros

A rare delicacy out on the open plains.

INGREDIENTS:
4 dozen fresh littleneck or cherrystone clams
8 garlic cloves
3 tablespoons olive oil
¼ cup water
1 pound linguini

½ cup (olive or canola) oil
2 tablespoons dried minced onion

EQUIPMENT:
Large clam pot with lid
Large pot

Wash the clams. Chop the garlic cloves and simmer half of the garlic in 3 tablespoons of olive oil in the clam pot for 2 minutes. Add the water and clams to clam pot. Cover the pot, raise the heat, and bring to a boil. Lower the heat and simmer until the shells open.

While the clams are cooking, cook the linguini in separate pot (about 8 to 10 minutes on high). Drain fully and return to the pot. Saute the rest of the garlic, minced onion, a half cup of oil, and pasta over low heat. Remove the clams from the shells and stir into the pasta. Serves 4 to 6.

Artichoke Uprising

(*Allegheny Uprising*, 1939)

There will be no up-rising from the table until all these artichokes have been eaten! Thanks to Paul "the Stuffer" Swindell for this recipe.

INGREDIENTS:
- 2 *large artichokes*
- 1 *cup Italian bread crumbs*
- ½ *cup Parmesan cheese*
- ½ *cup extra virgin olive oil*
- 2 *tablespoons garlic powder*
- 1 *tablespoon onion powder*
- 4 *tablespoons dried oregano*
- *Pinch of salt and fresh ground pepper*

EQUIPMENT:
Large bowl
Steamer

Clip the tips off the artichoke leaves and cut off the stems. Press the crown of each artichoke down on the countertop to open the leaves, and set aside.

Preheat the steamer. In a large bowl, add the bread crumbs and oil and mix together. Then add the salt, pepper, cheese, garlic, onion, and oregano. Mix all ingredients together. Stuff the mixture between the artichoke leaves and place the stuffed artichokes in the steamer for 45 minutes to an hour, or until leaves pull apart easily. Let cool for 10 minutes, then serve.

The War Wagon

Cast: John Wayne, Kirk Douglas, Howard Keel, Robert Walker,
    Keenan Wynn, Bruce Cabot, Joanna Barnes
Director: Burt Kennedy
Released by Universal Pictures (1967)

The "odd couple" teaming of John Wayne and Kirk Douglas continued with *The War Wagon,* their third collaboration in two years (the duo had previously costarred in *In Harm's Way,* 1965, and *Cast a Giant Shadow,* 1966). Despite being at opposite ends of the political spectrum— Duke was an arch-conservative while Douglas was a dyed-in-the-wool liberal—the actors enjoyed each other's company and respected each other's talent. Perhaps it was their obvious differences in real life that makes their onscreen chemistry so terrific.

In *The War Wagon,* Wayne and Douglas are once again cast as friendly adversaries. This time they conspire to rob a crooked land baron of a fortune in stolen gold by attacking his armored car prototype, the War Wagon. The horse-drawn, steel-encased, heavily armed vehicle proves to be too much of an obstacle for even the likes of Wayne and Douglas, so they bribe an army of Indians to help them succeed. The film ends on an amusing and ironic note that is loosely based on *The Treasure of the Sierra Madre* (1948).

The War Wagon was vintage John Wayne and a highly enjoyable romp. To no one's surprise, it continued Duke's streak as one of the most popular box office attractions in the world.

Did You Know . . . ?

★ During the filming of *The War Wagon,* the Duke filmed a short appeal for the Will Rogers Hospital, which was screened in theaters prior to the main feature and now appears on the video *John Wayne: Behind the Scenes With the Duke* (see the end of this book for ordering information).

The Raw Wagon

If Taw had offered this sushi to the drivers of the war wagon, he might not have had to resort to gunplay.

INGREDIENTS:
- 1 *pound tilefish (or salmon, tuna, etc.)*
- *Juice of one lime*
- 4 *black mushrooms, dried*
- 3 *tablespoons sugar*
- 2 *tablespoons sake*
- ¼ *cup soy sauce*
- *Pinch horseradish*

RICE:
- ¼ *cup sugar*
- 1 *teaspoon salt*
- 1 *cup rice vinegar*
- 4 *cups cooked short grain rice*

EQUIPMENT:
- *3 medium bowls*
- *1 large plate*
- *2 medium saucepans*
- *Paper towels*
- *Serving plate*

To cook rice: place 4 cups of rice in a saucepan with 4 cups of water. Bring the water to a boil. Turn off the flame and cover the pot for 5 minutes.

Pour the boiling water over the cleaned and dressed fish, then quickly dunk them in ice water and pat dry with paper towels. Sprinkle the lime juice over the fish and refrigerate until ready to use.

Mix sugar and salt with the vinegar and toss well with the hot rice. Set aside and let cool to room temperature. Cover the mushrooms with hot water and soak for 30 minutes. Add 3 tablespoons of sugar, sake, and soy sauce, and simmer until all liquid is completely absorbed. Let cool to room temperature.

Scoop about 2 tablespoons of rice into your moistened hand and press into an oblong patty shape. Remove the mushrooms from the soy sauce mixture and set aside. Brush the top of the rice patty with the soy sauce mixture and smear on a pinch of horseradish. Cut the raw fish into slices, approximately the same size as the rice patties. Press the fish into the rice. Continue until all rice and fish are used. Slice the mushrooms into strips and place them on top of the fish. Serves 2 to 4.

Fondue Frontier

(*New Frontier,* also known as *Frontier Horizon,* 1939)

The settlers love this tasty cheese treat.

INGREDIENTS:
 1 split garlic clove
 2 cups white wine (Rhine,
     Riesling, or Chablis)
 1 pound Swiss cheese
 ½ cup all-purpose flour
     Several grains ground
     nutmeg
 6 tablespoons kirsch or cognac

 1 loaf day-old French bread
     Salt and pepper to taste

EQUIPMENT:
Double boiler or electric skillet
Medium bowl
Wooden spoon
Large resealable container

Rub the garlic around sides of the boiler or skillet. Heat the wine until almost boiling. Coat the cheese in the flour, mixed with the salt, pepper, and nutmeg. Add several pieces at a time to the wine, allowing each batch to melt over low to medium heat before adding more. Stir constantly with a wooden spoon until the fondue starts to bubble. When cool, place in a sealed container and freeze.

To serve: Thaw slightly and heat in a chafing dish. Add kirsch or cognac. If the fondue becomes too thick, stir in a little preheated wine.

To prepare the bread: Cut lengthwise in fourths and then each lengthwise into bite-size pieces. Use fondue forks to serve. Makes 4 cups.

I Cover the Nachos

(*I Cover the War*, 1937)

A tasty chip dip that's sure to generate newsreel footage. Thanks to our correspondent, Stephanie Hetlyn.

INGREDIENTS:
- 1 10-ounce package sharp Cheddar cheese
- 1 8-ounce package cream cheese
- 1 15-ounce can no-bean chili

Cayenne pepper and dried minced onion to taste
Nacho chips

EQUIPMENT:
Round casserole dish

Shred the Cheddar cheese, then soften the cream cheese. Spread the cream cheese as the bottom layer in the casserole dish. Spread a layer of chili on top of the cream cheese, then cover the chili with the shredded cheddar. Sprinkle with pepper and onion, if desired. Heat in a microwave about 7 to 10 minutes at medium-high setting, or until top layer of cheese is melted. Dig in with your favorite nacho chip. Serves 4 to 6.

The Shootist

Cast: John Wayne, Lauren Bacall, Ron Howard, Richard Boone,
Scatman Crothers, Hugh O'Brian, Harry Morgan, Sheree North,
John Carradine, James Stewart
Director: Don Siegel
Released by Paramount Pictures (1976)

It's doubtful that John Wayne could have envisioned a more appropriate film on which to retire than *The Shootist,* a somber but superbly made western detailing the last days in the life of a cancer-stricken gunfighter. Determined to go out in a blaze of glory, his John Bernard Books dies a heroic death, ridding a town of some of its least desirable inhabitants in the process. There is a poignancy to the film that is made even more pronounced because of the parallels between Duke and his onscreen character. Both showed great dignity in the face of certain death from cancer.

Despite the fact that Duke was surrounded by many of his former costars (each of whom seemed to sense this would be their last opportunity to work with him), *The Shootist* was not a pleasant experience for the legendary actor. He was in bad health and irritable. He also locked horns with director Don Seigel, who could be equally stubborn. Wayne finished the film exhausted and, although professed to be developing another film called "Beau John," seemed to sense this would be his cinematic swan song.

Artistically, *The Shootist* is "one of the great films of our time"—in the words of the *Variety* review. Wayne's performance ranks among his best, and he is ably supported by a terrific cast. It makes one almost weep with gratitude to watch the Duke and such old pros as Lauren Bacall, Richard Boone, John Carradine, and Jimmy Stewart share the screen one last time in a vehicle worthy of their talents. Although the Duke would suffer from declining health until his death in 1979, he could take pride that *The Shootist* ended his distinguished career on a high note.

Did You Know . . . ?

★ *The Shootist* was nominated for an Oscar in the category of Art Direction.

The Shrimpist

Delicious shrimp kabobs that you can braise on your grill or broil in your oven. Thanks to "Sharpshootin'" Jim Hamilton.

INGREDIENTS:
- 1 *pound raw shrimp, cleaned and deveined*
- 1 *16-ounce can pineapple chunks*
- 1 *tablespoon cooking oil*
- 1 *teaspoon lemon juice extract*
- ¼ *cup pineapple juice*
- ¼ *teaspoon dried garlic*
- 1 *pinch dill*
- 1 *teaspoon sesame seeds*
- *Salt and pepper to taste*

EQUIPMENT:
Metal shishkebob skewers
Large bowl with lid (big enough to place skewers in)

Combine all ingredients except the shrimp and pineapple chunks in the bowl. Alternately poke the shrimp and pineapple chunks onto skewers. Place the skewers into the bowl, cover, and place in the refrigerator. Marinate for at least an hour, turning the bowl completely over and back several times to mix everything up. Place the skewers on a hot grill or in a broiler, turning often, for 5 to 10 minutes. Serves 6.

A STAMPEDE OF
SOUPS AND STEWS

Wayne
on
wheels!

JOHN WAYNE

"McQ"

A BATJAC AND LEVY · GARDNER PRODUCTION

CO-STARRING
EDDIE ALBERT · DIANA MULDAUR · COLLEEN DEWHURST · CLU GULAGER · DAVID HUDDLESTON · AL LETTIERI as "Santiago"

TECHNICOLOR® · PANAVISION® · Music by ELMER BERNSTEIN · Executive Producer MICHAEL A. WAYNE · Written and Co-Produced by LAWRENCE ROMAN

Produced by JULES LEVY and ARTHUR GARDNER · Directed by JOHN STURGES · From Warner Bros. A Warner Communications Company

PG PARENTAL GUIDANCE SUGGESTED

McQ

Cast: John Wayne, Eddie Albert, Diana Muldar, Colleen Dewhurst,
   Clu Gulager, David Huddleston, Al Lettieri
Director: John Sturges
Released by Warner Bros. (1974)

By 1974, the traditional western was considered by Hollywood all but dead. Indeed, John Wayne's two most recent contributions to the genre—*The Train Robbers* and *Cahill: U.S. Marshall* (both 1973)—were both box office disappointments. Duke therefore decided to switch gears and capitalize on the latest trend: hard-hitting cop films. Cast as Lon McQ, a bull-headed detective, Wayne finds himself in hot water when he is framed by crooks for the theft of a large cache of heroin from police headquarters. McQ must go it alone to crack the case.

The idea of Wayne making a career change in his mid-sixties seemed ludicrous to many critics, and, indeed, all but a few heaped scorn on *McQ.* An objective look, however, finds this to be a superior thriller, with Wayne surprisingly effective as a contemporary cop. He is surrounded by a solid cast, with Eddie Albert, Al Lettieri, and Colleen Dewhurst especially good. The film gave Duke a long-awaited opportunity to work with director John Sturges, whose credits included such classics as *The Great Escape* (1963) and *Gunfight at O.K. Corral* (1957).

McQ featured some excellent action set pieces, including an exciting car chase on the Olympic Peninsula near Seattle.

Although hardly a blockbuster at the box office, it did prove quite popular with Wayne's fans. Considering the mindless gore of cop movies of recent years, *McQ* looks positively inspired by comparison.

Did You Know . . . ?

★ John Wayne was originally offered the role of *Dirty Harry* (1971) that would go to Clint Eastwood (after Frank Sinatra also passed). Wayne declined due to the harsh language in the film. He would later admit he regretted his decision.

McStew

Nice to come home to after a hard day of car chases and gunplay.

INGREDIENTS:
- 1 *pound cubed boneless beef*
- 2 *tablespoons shortening*
- ½ *can beef consomme (or 1 cup beef bouillon)*
- 1 *pound can stewed tomatoes*
- 3 *medium potatoes, cubed*
- 1 *cup fresh or frozen peas*
- 1 *bay leaf*
- 2 *tablespoons tapioca*
- ¼ *cup bread crumbs*
- ½ *cup (or to taste) whole tiny onions or chopped fresh onions*
- 1 *8-ounce can green beans (do not drain)*
- 3 *carrots, sliced*
- 1 *tablespoon dark brown sugar*
- *Salt and pepper to taste*

EQUIPMENT:
Large roaster or Dutch oven

Brown the beef cubes on all sides in the bottom of the pot in the shortening and add the rest of the ingredients to the pot. Cover and bake at 250° F. for 7 hours. Serves 2 to 4.

The Big Stampeasoup

(*The Big Stampede,* 1932)

Nothing like a hearty bowl of pea soup after a hard day of bringing cattle rustlers to justice.

INGREDIENTS:
- 1 *cup dried split peas*
- 3 *quarts water*
- 1 *ham bone*
- 1 *tablespoon dried minced onion*
- 3 *tablespoons salted butter*
- 3 *tablespoons all-purpose flour*
- 1 *teaspoon salt*
- 2 *cups milk*
- *Pepper to taste*

EQUIPMENT:
Large pot
Medium pot

Soak the peas overnight in water, drain them in the morning, and cover them with 3 quarts of water in the large pot. Add the ham bone and onion, and cook them 45 minutes on medium or until they are soft.

Melt the butter and stir the flour in the medium pot until they are well blended and smooth. Add the salt, pepper to taste, and the milk, and cook, stirring occasionally, until the mixture thickens. Combine milk mixture with the peas and ham bone and cook over low flame until the soup is rather thick, about one half-hour. Serves 2 to 4.

Ladle of the Crowds

(*Idol of the Crowds*, 1937)

You'll shoot and score with this delicious turkey chowder.

INGREDIENTS:
 2 cups cubed, pared potatoes
 1 10-ounce package frozen
   baby lima beans
 ½ cup chopped onions
 ½ cup sliced celery
 ¼ teaspoon salt
 2 cups water
1½ cups cooked turkey
 1 16-ounce can crushed
   tomatoes
 ½ teaspoon poultry seasoning

 ¼ teaspoon garlic salt
 1 (10-ounce approx.) can
   condensed cream of
   chicken soup
 ⅛ teaspoon pepper
 ½ cup cheddar cheese,
   shredded

EQUIPMENT:
3-quart saucepan
Medium to large bowl

In the saucepan, combine the potatoes, beans, onion, celery, and salt. Blend the water with the condensed soup, then add to the vegetables. Cover and cook for 45 minutes over low heat or until the vegetables are tender. Add the undrained tomatoes, chopped turkey, and all remaining ingredients. Cover and simmer 15 minutes. Serves 8.

McLintock!

Cast: John Wayne, Maureen O'Hara, Yvonne De Carlo,
Patrick Wayne, Chill Wills
Director: Andrew V. McLaglen
Released by United Artists (1963)

One of Duke Wayne's most popular films, *McLintock!* was a major box office hit and a consistent top ratings-earner in its many airings on network television. This was due almost entirely to Wayne's teaming once again with Maureen O'Hara. Here they play an estranged couple who try to deny their mutual attraction to each other. O'Hara is the prim and proper snob who supposedly detests her wild and woolly husband, played by the Duke. Predictably, the two have a spirited—and very public—battle royale in which Wayne "tames" his wife and coerces her into returning to him. The extended sequence depicting the fighting McLintocks calls to mind similar scenes in *The Quiet Man* (1952) and *North to Alaska* (1960). There's nothing very original in *McLintock!,* but Wayne and O'Hara are so obviously enjoying themselves that it is difficult not to get swept up in the spirit of the proceedings.

McLintock! also boasts the famous sequence in which Wayne and O'Hara—along with virtually the entire town—end up brawling in a mud pit. It's predictable, but irresistible, fun. The movie also benefits from a sterling supporting cast and a catchy theme song. The movie may not be art, but it remains one of Wayne's most popular films.

Did You Know . . . ?

★ With *McLintock!,* Andrew V. McLaglen (son of actor and Wayne costar Victor McLaglen) made his debut as director. He would also direct the Duke in such films as *Chisum* (1970), *The Undefeated* (1969), *Hellfighters* (1968), and *Cahill: United States Marshall* (1973).

McLinstock!

A beef stew for every rancher.

INGREDIENTS:
- 2 *pounds chuck steak*
- 1 *tablespoon olive oil*
- 1 *quart potatoes (peeled)*
- 1 *cup carrots*
- 1 *pound string beans*
- 1 *cup celery*
- ½ *cup diced onion*
- 1 *garlic clove*

- 1 *16-ounce can tomato sauce*
- 1 *teaspoon salt*
- ½ *teaspoon pepper*

EQUIPMENT:
Cutting board
Large stew pot

Dice the steak into approximately 1½-inch cubes. Cut up the potatoes, carrots, and beans into ½-inch pieces, then dice the celery, onion, and garlic. Brown the meat in olive oil in a stew pot. Slowly add the celery, onions, garlic, salt, and pepper, and saute with the meat approximately 5 to 10 minutes. Add the tomato sauce and one cup of water. Cover and simmer for 1 hour. Add the remaining ingredients. Cover and cook over medium heat until the carrots are tender, about 10 minutes. Serves 6.

Red River

Cast: John Wayne, Montgomery Clift, Joanne Dru, Walter Brennan,
Coleen Gray, John Ireland, Noah Beery, Jr.
Director: Howard Hawks
Released by United Artists (1948)

Widely recognized as a prairie version of *Mutiny on the Bounty*, Howard Hawks's *Red River* still ranks as one of the screen's greatest westerns. With a final budget approaching a then sizable $3 million, Hawks fashioned a thinking man's epic in which John Wayne gave one of the most towering performances of his career. The film was important to the Duke because up to that point, critics had noted that most of his better performances had been under the direction of John Ford. With the universal praise he gained for his portrayal of the harsh and often unsympathetic trail boss Tom Dunson, Wayne had proven that his talent extended beyond the Ford films. (Upon seeing the film, Ford quipped, "I didn't know the S.O.B could act!")

Red River cast Wayne opposite up-and-coming Broadway star Montgomery Clift (who Wayne feared would be too lightweight to share the screen with him) as his estranged adopted son who takes over the cattle drive when Dunson's methods prove too cruel. Although the Duke and Clift never learned to like each other, both admitted their onscreen

"Say, where do you think we might rustle up some croutons for our soup?"

chemistry was excellent. The film was a rousing box office and critical success, and helped establish the Duke as a leading man capable of playing mature and complex roles.

Did You Know . . . ?

★ Howard Hawks originally wanted Gary Cooper for the role of Tom Dunson and Cary Grant for the part of Cherry Valance, a gunman who was relegatod to a supporting character when Grant declined the role. (The part was ultimately played by John Ireland.)

Red River Soup

A tasty Tex-Mex–style soup, with a scarlet color reminiscent of Missouri's Red River.

INGREDIENTS:
- 1 *pound lean ground beef*
- 1 *10-ounce can tomatoes*
- 1 *14½-ounce can stewed tomatoes*
- 1 *17-ounce can cream corn*
- 1 *16-ounce can mixed vegetables*
- 1 *13-ounce can Spanish rice*
- ½ *cup chopped onion*
- 1 *packet taco seasoning mix*

EQUIPMENT:
Large stock pot with lid

Brown the ground beef and onion in the pot. Drain the grease thoroughly. Add the canned ingredients, stirring in thoroughly. Cover and simmer for about an hour, stirring occasionally. Add taco seasoning to taste. Serves 4 to 6.

The Sea Chase

(The Sea Chase, 1955)

The seafood and vegetables chasing each other around your bowl is reminiscent of the chase between Ehrlich and Napier.

INGREDIENTS:

1 *celery stalk*
1 *medium onion*
1 *leek*
1 *carrot*
1 *small fennel root*
1 *garlic clove*
1 *bay leaf*
   Pinch of thyme leaves
½ *teaspoon Spanish saffron*
¼ *cup olive oil*
1 *cup fish stock*
1 *cup white wine*
1 *pound cod, or other white fish*

2 *large tomatoes*
1 *1-pound lobster*
1 *dozen medium shrimp*
1 *dozen clams or mussels*
½ *pound bay scallops*
   Chopped (fresh or dried)
   parsley
1 *lemon*
   Salt and pepper to taste

EQUIPMENT:
Cutting board
Soup pot with lid
Medium pot

Chop the celery, onion, leek, carrot, fennel, and garlic; crumble the bay leaf. Add them all to a large soup pot, along with the thyme, saffron, salt, pepper, and olive oil. Simmer for 10 minutes, tightly covered.

Peel and chop the tomatoes; add to the soup pot along with the fish stock, wine, and fish, and simmer 10 more minutes.

Boil the lobster in a separate pot, then scrub it, split it, and remove the dark vein, cut it up into sections, and set it aside. Peel and clean the shrimp; clean the clams or mussels. Add clams or mussels to the pot. Cook until the shellfish open, about 5 to 10 minutes. Then add shrimp and scallops. When the shrimp rise to the surface, remove from heat and serve.

Just prior to serving, add the lobster pieces, sprinkle with parsley and juice from the lemon, and heat through. Makes 6 servings.

The Barbarian and the Geisha

Cast: John Wayne, Eiko Ando, Sam Jaffe, So Yamamura
Director: John Huston
Released by Twentieth Century–Fox (1958)

These two rules should have been readily apparent in Hollywood by 1958:

1. Never cast John Wayne in a role which requires an accent.
2. Never cast John Wayne in a role which requires him to wear a stovepipe hat.

Alas, the great director John Huston ignored the latter rule in his ambitious but misguided big-budget film, *The Barbarian and the Geisha.* Wayne was cast as Townsend Harris, America's first foreign consul to Japan and the man credited with ending that nation's isolation from the rest of the world. If the process was as dull as depicted onscreen, chances are the Japanese would still be recluses.

The Duke and Huston became enemies as soon as production started. Wayne accused Huston of being sloppy and indecisive, while Huston shot back that Wayne was trying to make an important historical story into a thinly disguised, action-packed western. Both men barely

 45

spoke on the set, but Huston succeeded in removing most of the fisticuffs and concentrating on a chaste love story between Townsend Harris and a local geisha girl played by Eiko Ando (who was acting as Huston's real life "geisha" offscreen, much to the Duke's annoyance).

By the time the movie opened, both the director and the star knew they had a bomb on their hands. Wayne and Huston blamed each other for ruining the final cut, and the studio took a loss on the $3.5 million production. Wayne correctly assumed that his fans wanted to see him in action, not riding about dressed up like a dime-store version of Abe Lincoln.

Did You Know . . . ?

★ The original title of the film was the equally uninspired *The Townsend Harris Story*. The title was changed to *The Barbarian and the Geisha* over John Huston's objections.

The Barbarian and the Geisha's Stew

Contrary to popular belief, Okichi did not whip up this dish in Harris's stovepipe hat! Thanks for this recipe to Judith Hamilton-san.

INGREDIENTS:
- 1½ *pounds stew meat (beef or pork), cut into cubes*
- 2 *tablespoons oil*
- 2–3 *carrots, shredded*
- 1 *large onion*
- 1 *8-ounce can tomato sauce*
- ½ *cup water*
- ¼ *cup dark brown sugar, packed*
- ¼ *cup white vinegar*
- 1 *tablespoon Worcestershire sauce*
- 1 *teaspoon salt*
- 2 *teaspoons corn starch*
- 1 *tablespoon water*
- 1 *pound noodles*

EQUIPMENT:
3-quart saucepan

Boil noodles according to package directions. Brown the meat in oil in the saucepan. Add the carrots, onions, tomato sauce, a half cup of water, brown sugar, vinegar, Worcestershire, and salt. Cover and cook over low heat, about 1 hour.

Blend the corn starch with 1 tablespoon of water. Add to the stew. Cook until thickened and bubbly, about 5 minutes on medium. Serve over noodles. Serves 4 to 6.

Ladle and Garlic

(*Lady and Gent,* 1932)

Before kissing her boyfriend, a lady who's had this garlic soup should pop a breath mint!

INGREDIENTS:
- ¼ cup dried, minced garlic
- 1 teaspoon white pepper
- ½ teaspoon ground thyme
- 1 bay leaf
- 5 cups chicken broth

- 2 slices sourdough bread
- 2 tablespoons extra virgin olive oil

EQUIPMENT:
Soup pot with lid

Combine the garlic, pepper, thyme, bay leaf, and broth in the pot. Bring to a boil, then cover and simmer for 7 minutes. Toast the bread, then crumble it into the soup. Bring to a rolling boil, stirring occasionally.

Remove from heat. Pour the olive oil on the soup and serve. Serves 2 to 3.

Corn to the West

(*Born to the West,* 1938)

A corn chowder you were born to enjoy!

INGREDIENTS:
1 *tablespoon salted butter*
1 *tablespoon refined flour*
½ *teaspoon onion (finely grated)*
    Dash white pepper
1 *cup milk*

1 *15-ounce can creamed corn*
1 *15-ounce can corn niblets*
2 *tablespoons bacon bits*

EQUIPMENT:
Medium saucepan

Drain water from the corn niblets. In the saucepan, melt the butter, then stir in the flour, onions, and pepper. Stir constantly until well blended. Add milk, and continue to cook over medium heat until thickened, about one minute, stirring constantly. Add the corn. Heat through (about 3 minutes on medium flame). Garnish with bacon bits. Serves 2 to 4.

Stew Frontier

(*New Frontier,* 1935)

A zesty Tex-Mex–style stew worth fighting for.

INGREDIENTS:
- 5 dried red chilies (5-inches long)
  Salted butter (pat)
- 1 pound lean pork
- 1 teaspoon dried oregano (ground)

½ teaspoon garlic powder
Salt to taste

EQUIPMENT:
Medium saucepan with cover
Large skillet with cover
Blender or food processor

Remove the stems and seeds from the chilies and place them in the saucepan. Cover with water and bring to a boil over medium heat, then simmer, covered, for 25 minutes.

Grease the bottom of the skillet well with butter. Cut the pork into cubes. Drop them into the skillet and saute on high until all sides are well browned.

In a blender or processor, drop half of the cooked chilies and enough water to make a puree the consistency of ketchup—but do not discard the rest of the water! Scrape the puree into the skillet along with the meat. Use the rest of chilies to make another batch of puree and again add to the meat. Then add the salt, oregano, and garlic. Stir together and add chili water to cover the mixture. Replace the saucepan lid, and cook over medium heat for 30 minutes, stirring occasionally. Serves 4.

The Oniony Trail

(*The Lonely Trail,* 1936)

Even carpetbaggers can't resist onion soup!

INGREDIENTS:
  3 tablespoons salted butter
  3 large onions
  1 tablespoon all-purpose flour
  ½ teaspoon salt
     Dash black pepper
  5 cups beef broth
  4 thick slices French bread
  4 tablespoons grated Parmesan
     cheese

  4 slices mozzarella cheese
     (about 4 to 6 ounces)

EQUIPMENT:
Soup pot
4 individual, oven-safe soup
  bowls
Toaster oven

Thinly slice the onions. Melt the butter in the pot, then add the onions and cook slowly, stirring occasionally, until golden. Sprinkle on the flour and stir for a few minutes. Season with salt and pepper. Add the broth, stirring occasionally. Bring to a boil, then lower the heat, and let the soup simmer, partially covered, for 30 minutes.

Preheat the oven to 450° F. Toast the slices of bread in a toaster oven. Place them in the bottom of individual bowls. Sprinkle the bread with Parmesan, pour the broth mixture over the bread, and top with a slice of mozzarella. Place it in the oven until the cheese melts and browns slightly. Serves 4.

SIDEWINDER SALADS

"You're such a dear for making that Roughage Romance for me."

Pepper Canyon

(*Paradise Canyon*, 1935)

Counterfeiters would risk being caught at the refrigerator to enjoy this chilled, roasted pepper salad. Thanks for this recipe to "Peppery" Paul Swindells.

INGREDIENTS:
- 4 large red peppers
- ½ teaspoon garlic powder
- 1 tablespoon balsamic vinegar
- 1 tablespoon dried oregano
- ½ tablespoon dried basil
- ½ tablespoon dried parsley
- ½ cup extra virgin olive oil
- Dash salt and pepper

EQUIPMENT:
- Cutting board
- Cookie sheet
- Resealable bowl

Cut the peppers into quarters lengthwise. Broil with skin side up on a cookie sheet, about 4 inches from the broiler flame. When the skin turns black, run the peppers under cold water and remove the skin. Place them in a large sealable container, and add the remaining ingredients. Replace the lid, shake the bowl, and let chill in the refrigerator for about 2 hours.

Three Grills Tossed

(*Three Girls Lost*, 1931)

Fortunately, this lost chicken has been found, and it's the main ingredient of this spicy, cold salad. Thanks to the good girl, Judy Hamilton, for this recipe.

INGREDIENTS:

- 3–4 chicken breasts, boned and skinned
- 2 teaspoons cooking oil or Pam
  Salad greens (romaine lettuce, red cabbage, cucumber)
  Fresh mixed veggies (snow peas, cut asparagus, broccoli florets, thinly sliced carrots)
- 1 12-ounce can chick peas
- 1 tomato
- 1 small onion (optional)
  Olive oil (optional)
  Balsamic vinegar (optional)

SPICE MIX:

- 2½ tablespoons paprika
- 1 tablespoon salt
- 1 tablespoon onion powder
- 2 tablespoons garlic powder
- 1 tablespoon thyme
- 1 tablespoon ground red pepper
- 1 tablespoon ground black pepper
- ½ tablespoon chili powder

EQUIPMENT:
Small airtight container
Skillet
Cutting board
Steamer
Large bowl

Combine all the ingredients for the spice mix and store in an airtight container.

Heat the skillet and add oil. Pound the chicken breasts lightly on the cutting board and moisten with a few drops of water. Sprinkle the fronts and backs with the spice mix (the hotter you like your chicken, the more spice you use). Cook the chicken fully, turning once, cook 5 to 7 minutes on each side over medium flame. Set aside to cool, then slice into strips.

Cut up the greens, tomato, and cukes. Steam and cool the asparagus, broccoli, snow peas, and carrots. Combine the veggies and salad greens, and add the cut-up chicken. Toss with salad dressing (we suggest a mixture of balsamic vinegar and olive oil). Serves 4 to 6.

Note: Use any of your favorite greens and vegetables.

Roughage Romance

(*Rough Romance*, 1930)

Homemade dressings sure to romance any salad.

FRENCH

INGREDIENTS:
- 1 cup canned tomato soup
- ½ cup salad oil
- ¼ cup white vinegar
- 2 tablespoons sugar
- 1 tablespoon onion, finely chopped
- 2 teaspoons dry mustard
- ¼ teaspoon salt
- ¼ teaspoon pepper

EQUIPMENT:
Cruet or other covered container

Place all the ingredients in the container and chill. Shake well before using. Yield about 2 cups.

ITALIAN

INGREDIENTS:
- ½ cup finely chopped onion
- 1 garlic clove
- ¼ cup sugar
- 1 cup red wine vinegar
- 1 cup olive oil
- 1 cup ketchup
- 2 teaspoons salt
- 1 teaspoon dry mustard
- 1 teaspoon paprika
- 1 teaspoon dried oregano ground

EQUIPMENT:
Resealable container with lid
Strainer

Chop the garlic until minced. Combine all ingredients in the container, attach the lid, and shake until mixed. Strain to remove most of the onion and garlic. Refrigerate for 2 hours. Shake well before using. Yield about 2 cups.

California Straight A-Head

(*California Straight Ahead,* 1937)

A unique and satisfying stuffed head of lettuce.

INGREDIENTS:
1 *small head iceberg lettuce*
2 *3-ounce packages cream cheese*
⅓ *cup crumbled blue cheese*
¼ *cup mayonnaise*
2 *tablespoons finely chopped green pepper*
2 *tablespoons finely chopped red onion*
2 *tablespoons finely chopped fresh chives*

2 *tablespoons finely chopped walnuts*
1 *teaspoon Worcestershire sauce*
   Dash of pepper sauce

EQUIPMENT:
Medium bowl
Paper towels
Foil

Core the lettuce and hollow out the center, leaving a shell about one inch thick. Wash and drain thoroughly. Beat the cream cheese, blue cheese, and mayonnaise until smooth. Add the pepper, onion, chives, walnuts, Worcestershire, and pepper sauces. Pack in the center of the lettuce. Wrap the lettuce in wet paper towels, then in foil. Chill 2 hours or longer. Cut into wedges to serve. Serves 4 to 6.

Legend of the Tossed

(*Legend of the Lost,* 1957)

This zesty tomato salad is a real refreshing treat, especially after traveling across the blistering sands of the Sahara. Thanks to Ginny Emaus for this recipe.

INGREDIENTS:
2 *large tomatoes*
1 *large onion*
1 *garlic bulb*
⅓ *cup olive oil*
1 *teaspoon fresh oregano*

1 *teaspoon fresh basil*
Salt and pepper to taste

EQUIPMENT:
Cutting board
Resealable bowl

Cut up the tomatoes into chunks. Chop the onion and garlic cloves into small pieces. Put all the chopped items into the bowl. Add the olive oil, oregano, basil, salt, and pepper. Stir, then reseal the bowl. Refrigerate for 1 hour. Serves 4 to 6.

Two-Fisted Slaw

(*Two-Fisted Law,* 1932)

Don't pick up cole slaw with your fists, use a fork or spoon instead!

INGREDIENTS:
- 1 medium head of cabbage
- 1 medium onion
- 2 tablespoons cider vinegar
- ¼ cup plain yogurt
- ¼ cup mayonnaise
- 1 tablespoon sugar

- ½ teaspoon salt
- ¼ teaspoon black pepper
- ½ teaspoon dry dill

EQUIPMENT:
Small bowl
Resealable bowl or Ziploc bag

In a small bowl, mince the onion and set it aside. Shred the cabbage into thin pieces. Sprinkle in the vinegar, minced onion, black pepper, and sugar. Pour the mixture into a plastic bag or resealable bowl and refrigerate for at least an hour.

Mix the yogurt, mayonnaise, and salt. Add this to the chilled cabbage mixture. Mix thoroughly and reseal. Refrigerate for at least 2 hours. Sprinkle on the dill, mix together, and serve. Serves 6.

TEN-GALLON BEVERAGES

"Here, Colonel, have some more Hot Toddy!"

Jet Pilot

Cast: John Wayne, Janet Leigh, Jay C. Flippen, Paul Fix
Director: Josef von Sternberg
Released by Universal Pictures (1957)

Although John Wayne and Howard Hughes were enormously success-ful in their respective fields, it is ironic that two of their three screen ventures together (*The Conqueror,* 1956, and *Jet Pilot*) rank among the most embarrassing projects of both men's careers. (The third film, *Flying Leathernecks,* 1951—though mediocre—seems like high art compared to those clunkers).

Jet Pilot's bizarre history began when the film went into produc-tion in late 1949. Hughes, who was an avid aviation buff, sought to use the emergence of jet aircraft with a contemporary espionage thriller. He cast John Wayne as a tough-as-nails all-American fighter pilot who plays romantic cat-and-mouse games with Soviet pilot Janet Leigh. The rela-tionship gives Wayne the opportunity to view Leigh in her bra and dazzle her with witty lines like "We *both* believe in uplifting the masses!"

The film cost a then astronomical $4 million, thanks to Hughes's perfectionism and inane insistence on having specific cloud formations in all the flying sequences. Ultimately, the movie was not released until

1957! By then, Hughes's modern jets appeared to be as contemporary as the contraption the Wright Brothers flew at Kitty Hawk. Appropriately, the film's ad campaign capitalized on "the atomic age"—because *Jet Pilot* laid a nuclear bomb at the box office.

As with *The Conqueror,* Hughes decided to punish the public and critics by withdrawing the movie from release. This act remains his greatest contribution to the cinema.

Did You Know . . . ?

★ By the time *Jet Pilot* was released, RKO—the studio which Howard Hughes owned—was no longer active as a studio. Universal had the dishonor of releasing the film.

Juice Pilot

A simple, delicious punch sure to soar out of the punch bowl.

INGREDIENTS:
2 46-ounce cans chilled
    Hawaiian Punch (any variety)
⅔ cup pineapple juice
1 6-ounce can frozen lemonade
    concentrate, thawed

12 ounces club soda, chilled

EQUIPMENT:
1½-quart ring mold
Punch bowl

The day before serving, pour one can of punch into the ring mold and freeze. Mix the remaining ingredients in a punch bowl. Just before serving, unmold the frozen punch and carefully place it in the punch bowl. Garnish with fresh fruit, if desired. Makes approximately a half gallon.

The Night Ciders

(*The Night Riders,* 1939)

A spiced cider that will warm the heart.

INGREDIENTS:
  1 *gallon natural apple cider*
  8 *whole cloves*
  1 *whole nutmeg*
  2 *cinnamon sticks*
  ½ *cup (packed) dark brown*
    sugar
    Pinch of sugar

EQUIPMENT:
Large pot

Put all the ingredients in a large pot, bring to a boil over medium heat, and simmer for 15 minutes. Strain and serve.

Blood Alley

Cast: John Wayne, Lauren Bacall, Paul Fix, Joy Kim
Director: William Wellman
Released by Warner Bros. (1955)

If you can believe that John Wayne can escape from a Red Chinese prison by overpowering a guard, donning his uniform, and walking through dozens of enemy troops without arousing suspicion, then *Blood Alley* is your kind of movie—and we also have a bridge in Brooklyn we would like to sell you. This overblown, big-budget adventure has more corn than the state of Iowa.

Wayne is a tough ferryboat captain who is persuaded to risk life and limb to smuggle a group of refugees from Red China into Hong Kong. This is one of those offensive epics in which many of the ethnic roles are played by Caucasians. One understands why the Duke didn't object, after all, it was his idea to play Genghis Khan in *The Conqueror* (1956)!

Despite some nice location scenery and the sultry presence of Lauren Bacall, *Blood Alley*—like the ferry Wayne steers in the film—is hopelessly off course.

Did You Know . . . ?

★ Robert Mitchum was originally cast as the star of the film. When he openly feuded with director William Wellman, John Wayne signed on to take his place.

Blood Alley Punch

A hot cranberry punch that warms souls from here to Hong Kong.

INGREDIENTS:
- 3 pints cranberry juice cocktail
- 2 cups orange juice
- 2 tablespoons lemon juice extract
- 2 cups sugar
- 3 cinnamon sticks
- 1 teaspoon dried cloves
- 2 quarts water

EQUIPMENT:
Medium to large pot

Combine all the ingredients in the pot; bring to a boil. Simmer 1 to 2 minutes. Dilute with water. Serve hot. Makes 16 servings.

Hot Toddy!
(*Hatari!,* 1962)

Don't try to catch any big game (or drive a car, for that matter) while you indulge in this hot coffee treat. Thanks for this recipe to the zookeeper, Judith Hamilton.

INGREDIENTS:
- 8 teaspoons sugar
- 6 cups espresso or strong coffee
- 8 jiggers Irish whiskey
- ½ cup heavy cream

EQUIPMENT:
Small bowl
8 goblets

Whip the cream. Put a teaspoon of sugar in each goblet, then add enough coffee to dissolve the sugar. Add 1 jigger of whiskey to each goblet. Fill to within 1 inch of the brim with coffee. Add a dollop of whipped cream to each. Do not stir. Serve at once.

Hurricane Espresso

(*Hurricane Express,* 1932)

A strong mocha coffee sure to stoke your engine.

INGREDIENTS:
- ¼ cup sugar
- 2 squares unsweetened chocolate
- 2 cups double-strength hot coffee
- 2 cups heavy cream
- Dash of salt

EQUIPMENT:
- Blender
- Large saucepan

Cut the chocolate into pieces, combine with sugar, salt, and coffee in a blender. Process low for a few seconds, then continue to process on high until smooth. Remove the feeder cap, and gradually add heavy cream. Replace the cap, and process only until the mixture is blended, about 5 minutes.

Pour the mixture into the saucepan, heat over low heat until piping hot. Pour into mugs and top with whipped cream, if desired. Makes 6 servings.

*"After a long day on the set, there's nothing like a steaming cup
of Hurricane Espresso."*

Haunted Cold

(*Haunted Gold,* 1932)

Sherbet punch straight from the abandoned "cold" mine.

INGREDIENTS:
- ½ cup sugar
- 2 cups water
- 1 6-ounce can frozen concentrated lemonade
- 3 6-ounce cans frozen orange juice
- 1 quart ginger ale
- 1 quart club soda
- 1 4-ounce jar maraschino cherries
- 1 pint lemon (or raspberry) sherbet
- 1 quart gin (optional)

EQUIPMENT:
Punch bowl

Melt the sugar in water in the punch bowl. Add frozen lemonade concentrate and the orange juice, mix. Add the ginger ale, club soda, and cherries (their juice too!). Just as company arrives, spoon sherbet on top. Serves about 12.

HEARTY BREADS

The Elder boys search the horizon for their favorite buns.

The Sons of Katie Elder

Cast: John Wayne, Dean Martin, Earl Holliman, Michael Anderson, Jr.,
Martha Hyer, Jeremy Slate, Paul Fix, James Gregory,
George Kennedy, Dennis Hopper
Director: Henry Hathaway
Released by Paramount Pictures (1965)

With *The Sons of Katie Elder,* John Wayne returned to theater screens
for the first time since his lung cancer operation. Cynics predicted that
the Duke would not work again, and in the early stages of location filming in the high altitudes of Durango, Mexico, it appeared as though the
naysayers would be right. Duke was fighting for every breath, and his
old friend, director Henry Hathaway, had little sympathy. Henry felt that
when it came to filmmaking the best remedy was "business-as-usual."
Hathaway rode the Duke mercilessly, ignoring pleas from Wayne's stunt
double Chuck Roberson to stand in for the action sequences.

Despite the tribulations of bringing *Katie* to the screen, Duke could
savor the fact that the response was overwhelmingly good. Both critics
and audiences reacted favorably to the old-fashioned tale of four
estranged brothers who reunite for their mother's funeral, only to become
embroiled in a life-and-death plot to rob them of their inheritance. The
film featured considerable charisma between Wayne and his three
"brothers," Dean Martin, Earl Holliman, and Michael Anderson, Jr.

With box office tills brimming, the world knew that John Wayne was indeed back in the saddle.

Did You Know . . . ?

★ Two months after the August 1965 premiere of *Katie Elder,* the Duke's wife Pilar announced she was pregnant. In February 1966 their daughter Marisa was born, making Wayne a proud papa again—at age fifty-eight.

The Buns of Katie Elder

No, not those kinds of buns, rather, honey buns that make a great addition to any meal.

INGREDIENTS:
3 cups all-purpose flour
1 package active dry yeast
1 teaspoon salt
1 cup hot water
¼ cup vegetable oil

¼ cup honey
1 large egg

EQUIPMENT:
Mixer bowl
Muffin pans

Combine 2 cups of flour, the yeast, and salt in a mixer bowl. Add the water, oil, honey, and egg; beat until smooth, about 2 minutes.

Beat in the remaining flour by hand. Cover, let the mixture rise until it doubles in bulk (about 30 minutes).

Fill greased muffin pan wells half full. Let the rolls rise until they double in bulk (about 30 minutes). Bake at 400° F., about 10 to 12 minutes, or until golden brown. Makes 2 dozen buns.

Loaf of Jimmy Dolan

(*Life of Jimmy Dolan,* 1933)

This is Jimmy's banana walnut bread, but he'll let you have some.

INGREDIENTS:
- ¾ cup sugar
- ¼ cup shortening
- 2 large eggs
- 1 cup fresh banana
- 2 cups all-purpose flour, sifted
- 2 teaspoons baking powder
- ½ teaspoon salt
- ¼ teaspoon baking soda
- 1 cup chopped walnuts

EQUIPMENT:
Small bowl
Large bowl
Loaf pan (9 × 5 × 3 inches)

Mash the banana in the small bowl. Mix the sugar, shortening, and eggs in the large bowl; beat hard until their consistency is light. Blend in the banana. Add the remaining dry ingredients, beating until smooth. Stir in the walnuts. Pour into a greased loaf pan. Bake at 350° F. for 60 minutes, or until the top of the loaf is golden brown.

The Grain Robbers

(*The Train Robbers,* 1973)

Few people realize that the recipe for this whole-grain bread was also stolen from the train. Fortunately, Lane saved the day, and we can all enjoy this tasty bread.

INGREDIENTS:
1 package active dry yeast
1½ cups warm water
2 tablespoons salted butter
2 tablespoons dark molasses
1 tablespoon salt
1 large egg

1 cup whole-grain cereal
3½ cups all-purpose flour

EQUIPMENT:
Small bowl
Large mixing bowl
2-quart souffle dish

Dissolve the yeast in ½ cup of warm water. Beat the egg slightly and crush the cereal. Combine the remaining water, butter, molasses, salt, egg, and cereal. Add the yeast and beat well in mixer. Beat in 2½ cups of flour and continue to beat until the dough becomes elastic in consistency. Pour into well-buttered souffle dish. Cover and set aside to rise in a warm place until the bulk doubles.

Bake at 350° F. for 1¼ hours, or until golden brown. Allow to sit for 10 minutes, then remove from the pan and cool on a rack.

Big Jim McLain

Cast: John Wayne, Nancy Olson, James Arness
Director: Edward Ludwig
Released by Warner Bros. (1952)

An anti-Communist propaganda film, the script for *Big Jim McLain* reads like a love letter to Senator Joe McCarthy. At a time in which legalized witch hunts against Hollywood talent were being sanctioned by the U.S. government, Duke Wayne—a staunch advocate of the House Un-American Activities Committee—decided to put a human face on the stalwart defenders of the Constitution. The fact is that these well-intentioned but misguided politicians destroyed innocent lives and threatened to turn America into the type of Big Brother–dominated society they claimed to deplore.

Wayne plays a two-fisted HUAC investigator sent to Honolulu to break up a nest of Commies. There's a Red under every bed, all right, but Duke's more interested in getting under the covers with glamour girl Nancy Olson, to whom he whispers the immortal mating cry "You're comfy without the french fries!"

Despite some nice location photography, *Big Jim McLain* is as subtle as an atomic bomb, and just about as entertaining (the code name for Wayne's Hawaiian mission is—we kid you not—Operation Pineapple!). Fortunately, there are enough bad moments to immortalize the film in the Plan 9 From Outer Space Hall of Fame, in that the unintentional laughs prove to be adequate compensation for the stale plot and dialogue.

Did You Know . . . ?

★ Duke Wayne personally recommended his *Big Jim McLain* and *Hondo* (1953) costar Jim Arness to the producers of TV's *Gunsmoke.* Thanks to him, Arness made a lucrative career playing Marshal Matt Dillon. The Duke even filmed the introduction to the pilot episode.

Big Jim's Favorite Irish Soda Bread

It wasn't always easy for Big Jim to find good, old-fashioned soda bread in Hawaii, so he held on to his grandmother's recipe.

INGREDIENTS:
- 3 *cups all-purpose flour*
- ¼ *cup sugar*
- 1 *tablespoon baking powder*
- 1 *teaspoon salt*
- ¼ *cup shortening*
- 1 *tablespoon caraway seeds*
- ½ *cup raisins*
- 1 *large egg*
- 1¼ *cups buttermilk*

EQUIPMENT:
Small bowl
Large bowl
Bread pan (9 × 5 × 3 inches)

Preheat the oven to 400° F. Sift the baking soda and grease the bread pan. Add all dry ingredients to the large bowl and blend together. Beat the egg into the small bowl, then add the egg and buttermilk to the flour mixture. Knead the dough, then put it in the pan and cross the top with a knife. Bake for about 30 to 45 minutes, until golden brown.

(Put a small amount of water in the oven while the bread is baking to keep the bread soft and moist.)

Texas Cycorn

(*Texas Cyclone*, 1932)

A hearty corn bread for hearty heroes.

INGREDIENTS:
1½ cups cornmeal
½ cup self-rising flour
1 teaspoon baking powder
1 teaspoon sugar
½ teaspoon baking soda
⅓ cup shortening

1½ cups buttermilk
2 large eggs

EQUIPMENT:
Large bowl
Bread pan

Mix all ingredients in the bowl by beating vigorously for 30 seconds. Pour the mixture into a well-greased bread pan. Bake at 450° F. for 25 minutes, or until golden brown. Makes 8 to 10 servings.

ENTREES FROM THE CHUCKWAGON

Two legendary stars enjoying a chuckle after a delicious meal.

The Big Trail

Cast: John Wayne, Marguerite Churchill, El Brendel, Tully Marshall, Tyron Power, Sr.
Director: Raoul Walsh
Released by Twentieth Century–Fox (1930)

Director Raoul Walsh's 1930 western was a milestone in the career of John Wayne, as it represented the first big-budget film in which he had starred. John Ford discovered Wayne on the set while Wayne was working as a prop man and had given him bit parts and stuntwork. He urged Walsh to consider Wayne for his first starring role. *The Big Trail* was an ambitious, early talkie centering on the adventures of a group of pioneers who are heading into the great unknown of the American West, circa 1840. The movie provided some outstanding sequences depicting Indian attacks and other disastrous encounters with which the wagon train must cope.

Shot in the first wide-screen process (Grandeur), it was Walsh's dream to have specially equipped theaters show his epic in its full glory. Alas, this was not to be. The film was released during the Depression, when only a few theaters could afford to purchase the expensive equipment necessary to project the movie in its 70mm format. Instead, the vast majority of theaters showed the film in standard 35mm, making a nonevent of the financially plagued Fox studio's boast that *The Big Trail* would revolutionize the moviegoing experience. Consequently, despite generally favorable reviews, the film was a notorious flop at the box office. Wayne's recently blossoming career nosedived and he was relegated to starring in low-budget B movies until *Stagecoach* gave his career another boost in 1939.

Did You Know . . . ?

★ It was during the production of *The Big Trail* that the Duke reluctantly agreed to be billed as John Wayne for the first time. Studio executives thought the name Duke Morrison was too lightweight for their new star.

The Big Trail Ribs

The trail of barbecue sauce leads right to the chuckwagon and lots of happy settlers.

INGREDIENTS:
3–4 *pounds spareribs (beef or pork)*
1 *whole lemon*
1 *large onion*
1 *cup ketchup*
⅓ *cup Worcestershire sauce*
1 *teaspoon chili powder*

2 *dashes Tabasco sauce*
2 *cups water*
  Salt to taste

EQUIPMENT:
Shallow baking pan
Medium pot

Cut up the ribs and place them in the pan, meaty side up. Place a slice of onion and a slice of lemon on each piece. Roast in a 450° F. oven for 30 minutes.

Combine the remaining ingredients in the pot and bring to a boil. Pour the sauce over the ribs and continue to bake in a 350° F. oven until tender, about 45 minutes. Baste the ribs with sauce every 15 minutes. If the sauce gets too thick, add more water. Serves 4 to 6.

Wurst of the Divide

(*West of the Divide,* 1933)

Sausage and rice casserole, a favorite on the ranch.

INGREDIENTS:
- 1 *pound sausage (bratwurst or sweet Italian)*
- 2 *packages dry chicken noodle soup mix*
- ¾ *cup long grain rice*
- 4½ *cups water*
- 1 *large green pepper*
- 1 *celery stalk*
- 1 *large onion*
- *Dash paprika*
- ½ *cup slivered almonds*

EQUIPMENT:
2 small bowls
Large skillet
Large saucepan
2 2-quart casserole dishes

Chop the celery and pepper and set aside. Brown the sausage in the skillet. In the saucepan, combine the soup mix, rice, and water. Bring to a boil, then let simmer for 7 minutes or until most of the liquid is absorbed by the rice.

Mix the sausage with the rice mixture, then add the celery, pepper, onions, and paprika. Divide the mixture into 2 casseroles and top with slivered almonds. Bake at 350° F. for 1 hour. (You can also cover the casserole and freeze until needed.)

"Fill Your Hams, You Son of a Bitch!"

(*True Grit,* 1969)

Paraphrasing Rooster Cogburn's famous line, here's a ham and noodle casserole straight from Mattie's kitchen—with thanks to "Rooster" Judy Hamilton.

INGREDIENTS:

Large ham steak
1 *pound pasta shells*
1 *cup frozen peas*
¼ *stick salted butter*
¼ *cup Romano cheese*

Salt and pepper to taste

EQUIPMENT:
Large frying pan
Large pot

Prepare the peas according to directions. Boil the pasta for ten minutes on high and drain thoroughly. Cut the ham into small squares and brown them in the pan, 2 to 3 minutes on medium. Add the ham to the pasta, then stir in the remaining ingredients. Mix well and serve. Serves 2 to 4 cowboys.

In Harm's Way

Cast: John Wayne, Kirk Douglas, Patricia Neal, Tom Tryon,
Paula Prentiss, Henry Fonda, Jill Haworth, Brandon De Wilde,
Burgess Meredith
Director: Otto Preminger
Released by Paramount Pictures (1965)

*I*n *Harm's Way* is a significant film in John Wayne's career, as well as in his personal life. It is one of the rare occasions in which Wayne is an ensemble player among a cast of Hollywood heavyweights. He is very much a major presence in this tale about the aftermath of the attack on Pearl Harbor, but it is refreshing to see him take a back seat to some other seasoned pros, each of whom has an opportunity to shine in this ambitious epic. Following the filming, however, Wayne learned that he had lung cancer.

When it was announced that Wayne, Kirk Douglas, and Otto Preminger would collaborate for this large scale World War II film, the industry waited for the sparks to fly. The trio were diametrically opposed to each other's methods of filmmaking and politics. To everyone's surprise, the making of *In Harm's Way* turned out to be an exercise in mutual admiration. The result was a sobering, mature look at the early days of the campaign in the Pacific in the aftermath of the attack on Pearl Harbor.

Wayne plays a tough Naval officer who experiences humiliation but eventually triumphs in his leadership of the U.S. fleet, due to his tendency to throw away the rule book. Douglas is his somewhat manic first officer whose lack of judgment clouds an otherwise heroic career. The script succeeds in weaving a number of love stories and personal crises with the battle sequences, and a first-rate supporting cast makes this a completely believable and often moving drama. By all accounts, Wayne and Douglas worked well together and, in fact, would collaborate twice more in the next two years.

Wayne suffered from an unrelenting cough during filming, and it was shortly after shooting was completed that he discovered he had lung cancer. With his life in grave danger, doctors predicted that even if he survived a necessary lung removal operation, he would never work again. Duke proved 'em wrong, of course. He "licked the big C," and in no time at all was back in the saddle for *The Sons of Katie Elder.*

In Ham's Way

Smoked Ham Marsala, enjoyed by Allied officers the world over.

INGREDIENTS:
> *Smoked butt end of ham*
2 *cups Marsala wine*
2 *cups dark brown sugar*
1 *tablespoon dried mustard*
> *Pineapple slices*

Maraschino cherries

EQUIPMENT:
Covered pan or casserole
Small bowl

Place the ham in the pan, pour on Marsala wine, and cover. Cook for ½ hour in a 350° F. oven. Remove from the oven and score the ham along the top. Combine the mustard and sugar in a small bowl and press into the ham. Increase the oven temperature to 450° F. and put the ham back in the oven, uncovered. Bake for 15 minutes, continuously basting with wine juices from the pan. Decorate with cherries and pineapple. Serves 4 to 6.

The Quiet Man

Cast: John Wayne, Maureen O'Hara, Barry Fitzgerald, Ward Bond,
   Victor McLagen, Mildred Natwick, Francis Ford
Director: John Ford
Released by Republic Pictures (1952)

Now considered a true classic, *The Quiet Man* had a rocky road to the screen. John Ford had purchased the screen rights to the story (for $10!) some twenty years prior to filming and had long dreamed of traveling to Ireland—the land of his heritage—to direct this sentimental and humorous love story. Despite his box office track record, Ford could not find a major studio to back the project. Wayne convinced him to go to Republic, which had been a B movie studio trying to enter the ranks of A pictures. Studio boss Herbert Yates financed the film, but constantly clashed with Ford over the budget and running time. It was only after *The Quiet Man* won international acclaim—and Oscars for John Ford and for Best Picture—that Yates became a true believer. Ford never forgave Yates for his arrogance, and neither he nor Wayne worked for the studio again.

The Quiet Man finds Wayne as an American champion boxer who, haunted by the fact that he accidentally killed an opponent in the ring, attempts to forget his troubles by moving to a small, picturesque village in Ireland. Here, he falls in love with a fiery colleen, a development which leads to conflict with her bully of a brother. The cast was first rate, with Barry Fitzgerald, Ward Bond, and Victor McLaglen providing superb support for Wayne and stunningly beautiful leading lady Maureen O'Hara. The film benefits from Winston Hoch's fabulous cinematography and—in contrast to most of today's films—a leisurely pace and wonderfully rich dialogue. *The Quiet Man* proved that Duke Wayne didn't need a rifle or a horse to dominate the screen. The film was regarded as one of his major career achievements, and even today, millions of his fans devotedly watch it every St. Patrick's Day.

Did You Know . . . ?

★ When John Ford fell ill on the set, Duke Wayne directed some of the second unit scenes.

The Quiet Man's Corned Beef and Cabbage Dinner

Sean discovered this classic dish hidden in a kitchen drawer in the cottage in which he was born. Now, you can enjoy a piece of his heritage, too.

INGREDIENTS:
- *1 5-pound corned beef*
- *2 medium onions*
- *2 garlic cloves*
- *6 whole cloves*
- *2 bay leaves*
- *6 medium potatoes*
- *6 small carrots*
- *1 medium cabbage*

EQUIPMENT:
- *Cutting board*
- *Large stew pot with cover*

Place the corned beef in the pot and cover it with boiling water. Add the onion (sliced), garlic (minced), cloves, and bay leaves. Simmer for 5 hours, covered. Remove the meat. Add potatoes (peeled) and carrots (scraped). Boil, covered, for 10 minutes. Add the cabbage (cut into 6 wedges). Boil, covered, for 20 minutes. Slice the corned beef. Serves 6.

"There goes Red Will, runnin' off with all the corned beef!"

How the West Was Won

Cast: John Wayne, James Stewart, Henry Fonda, Debbie Reynolds,
   Gregory Peck, Richard Widmark, George Peppard
Directors: John Ford, George Marshall, Henry Hathaway
Released by Metro Goldwyn Mayer (1962)

The 1962 production of *How the West Was Won* was an epic in every sense of the word. It represented the high-water mark of Cinerama, the unique wide-screen process which presented a picture so large that it took three synchronized projectors to show it on a large, curved screen. In those days, the average cost of an epic film was approximately $3 million. Because of the expense of bringing a Cinerama production to completion, *West* cost a then astonishing $15 million. The film, which told of the settling of the American West, was so large in scope that it took three famed directors to bring to the screen: George Marshall, Henry Hathaway, and Duke Wayne's beloved mentor, John Ford. The cast was a virtual "who's who" of top stars, including James Stewart, Henry Fonda, Debbie Reynolds, Gregory Peck, Richard Widmark, and of course, John Wayne. Each of the actors took a drastic pay cut, accepting a fee of only $25,000. Wayne makes a brief but memorable appearance as cigar-chomping General Sherman, who convinces General Grant (Harry Morgan) not to despair and to stay in charge of the Union army.

Although the film was an enormous financial and artistic success (it was nominated for Best Picture), Cinerama's days were numbered. The cost and logistics of the process were too high for studios to sustain, and theaters could not afford the large investment in the special projectors that were required. In 1996, the Neon Theater in Dayton, Ohio, began showing the first Cinerama presentation of the film since its original release. It played to packed houses of movie enthusiasts who could once again relive the indescribable experience of a great film in the format in which it was meant to be seen.

Did You Know . . . ?

★ John Wayne and Henry Fonda both starred in two of the biggest hits of 1962—*How the West Was Won* and *The Longest Day*—yet never shared a scene together in either film.

How the Wurst Was Done

The West might never have been won if it weren't for hearty casseroles like this to satisfy pioneer families.

INGREDIENTS:
- 2 *pounds Italian pork sausage links*
- 1 *12-ounce can strained tomatoes*
- 1 *medium onion*
- 2 *small green peppers*
- 1 *8-ounce package elbow macaroni*
- *Grated Cheddar cheese*

EQUIPMENT:
Medium frying pan
Medium pot
Casserole dish

Cut up and brown the sausage. Cook the macaroni until tender (about 8 to 10 minutes) and strain. Grease the casserole dish and add the sausages and macaroni. Cut up the onion and pepper and add to casserole, along with the tomatoes. Top off with a sprinkled layer of grated cheese. Bake at 350° F. for 45 minutes, or until the cheese is slightly browned. Serves 2 to 4.

Ham Man's House

(*Hangman's House,* 1928)

Even the hangman loves this delicious casserole.

INGREDIENTS:
- 2 pounds fresh (or 2 9-ounce packages frozen) French-style green beans
- 3 tablespoons salted butter
- 3 tablespoons all-purpose flour
- 1 cup milk
- ½ teaspoon dried ground nutmeg
- 1 cup grated Cheddar cheese
- ⅔ cup coarsely cubed ham
- Salt and pepper to taste

EQUIPMENT:
- Medium pot
- 2-quart casserole dish

Cook the beans (in a microwave, 3 to 5 minutes on high, or on a stove top, 10 to 12 minutes in a cup of water over medium flame) until tender. Make the sauce by melting the butter and blending in the flour until a smooth paste is formed, and then slowly add milk. Cook until thickened. Add the nutmeg, salt, pepper, and cheese. Stir over low heat until the cheese is melted. Drain the beans and mix with the cheese sauce. Pour into a buttered casserole dish and top with the ham. Bake in a 350° F. oven for 20 to 25 minutes, or until brown and bubbly. Serves 4.

Roast Ham, Cowboy

(*Ride Him, Cowboy*, 1932)

A hearty, satisfying, roast ham entree.

INGREDIENTS:

*Precooked country ham
(8–10 pounds)*
8 *ounces Sauterne wine*
8–10 *garlic cloves*

EQUIPMENT:

*Large pot
Roasting pan with cover*

GLAZE:

*Mix 2 cups dark brown sugar
with enough Sauterne wine to
make a paste.*

Rinse the ham thoroughly in cool water. Place it in the pot and cover with cool water. Let boil. Remove the ham and place it in the roasting pan on an oven rack. Pour the wine over the ham. Cover the pan tightly and roast at 350° F. for 15 minutes per pound. Baste several times during cooking. Remove the skin and score the fat in a diamond shape. In each diamond, put one clove of garlic. Glaze the ham fat side up. Place the pan in a 450° F. oven for 15 minutes or until the glaze is brown. Remove to a platter, slice, and serve. Serves 4 to 6.

The Star Porker

(*The Star Packer,* 1934)

Make the deputies sit down long enough to enjoy these tasty chops. Thanks to "Marshal" Kathy Swindells.

INGREDIENTS:
1½ pounds pork chops (boneless
    or center cut)
    Lemon pepper
¼ cup Worcestershire sauce
1 teaspoon dry mustard
¾ cup water

EQUIPMENT:
Medium frying pan
Small bowl

Sprinkle lemon pepper on both sides of the chops. Brown over medium heat in a frying pan and drain. Mix the Worcestershire, mustard, and water together, pour over the chops in the pan and fry over low-medium heat for about one half-hour, or until fully cooked (juice runs clear).

    Goes well with white rice. Serves 2 to 4.

The Undefeathered

(*The Undefeated,* 1969)

Oven-fried chicken that will have them charging to the dinner table.

INGREDIENTS:
    2 cups crushed potato chips
    ½ teaspoon pepper
    ½ teaspoon curry powder
    2 large eggs
    ½ cup frozen orange juice
        concentrate
    ¼ cup water
2½–3 pounds chicken (cut up)

¼ cup melted butter (salted)
    Salt to taste

EQUIPMENT:
Blender and mixing bowl
Medium bowl
2-quart baking pan or casserole
    dish

Blend the potato chips, pepper, and curry powder in a blender. Beat the eggs and mix them with the orange juice and water. Lightly salt the chicken, then dip it into the egg mixture, and then the seasoned chips. Place the chicken side by side in the pan. Drizzle with melted butter and bake at 350° F. until tender, 40 to 45 minutes. Serves 4.

Turkey Along the Way

(*Trouble Along the Way,* 1953)

St. Anthony's famous turkey burgers. Thanks to "Quarterback" Paul Swindells for this recipe.

INGREDIENTS:
 1 *pound ground turkey*
 ½ *medium onion*
 3 *tablespoons Worcestershire*
   sauce
 2 *tablespoons soy sauce*
   Salt and pepper to taste

EQUIPMENT:
Large bowl
Medium frying pan or grill

Finely chop the onion. In a large bowl, mix the ground turkey and onion together thoroughly, then mix in Worcestershire and soy sauces. Form into patties and cook over medium heat until well browned (about six minutes). Add salt and pepper to taste. For a tasty treat, serve with a sliced tomato and lettuce, maybe even some Dijonnaise. Makes 4 good-size burgers.

Frying Feathernecks

(*Flying Leathernecks,* 1953)

A fighter squadron of chicken in pasta.

INGREDIENTS:
- *2 pounds chicken fillets*
- *1 pound ziti*
- *Italian bread crumbs*
- *2 large eggs*
- *Mrs. Dash Zesty seasoning*
- *Grated Parmesan cheese*
- *3 garlic cloves*
- *3 tablespoons minced onion (fresh or dried)*
- *Canola oil*

EQUIPMENT:
- *Cutting board*
- *Dinner plate*
- *Small bowl*
- *Medium frying pan*
- *Paper towels*
- *Large pot*

Rinse the chicken under running water. Cut into small strips, half the size of chicken fingers (be sure to remove all the skin, fat, cartilage, etc., from the meat). Beat the eggs and set them aside. Mince the garlic and set it aside. Pour a layer of bread crumbs onto the plate. Grease the frying pan with oil. Dip the chicken first in egg, then cover completely with bread crumbs and place in the frying pan. Fry the chicken pieces over low to medium heat until browned on all sides (about 5 minutes), then remove each piece from the pan and let the oil soak into the paper towels.

While the last few chicken pieces are cooking, cook the ziti, (boil over high heat for 8 to 10 minutes until tender) drain thoroughly, and put it back into the pot. When all the chicken has been cooked, dump the pieces back into the pot with the ziti, and add garlic and onion. Cook on very low flame, continuously tossing the mixture for about 5 minutes and sprinkling the grated cheese, Mrs. Dash, and oil (the pasta and meat will soak it all in, so you might have to keep adding seasoning and oil). Serve with additional grated cheese to taste. Serves 2 to 4.

Rooter Cogburn

Cast: John Wayne, Katharine Hepburn, Richard Jordan,
   Strother Martin
Director: Stuart Millar
Released by Universal Pictures (1975)

The long-awaited, highly anticipated sequel to the Duke's Oscar-winning film *True Grit* arrived in the fall of 1975—six years after the original movie was released. The film is notable only in that it provided Wayne with his one and only opportunity to star opposite Katharine Hepburn. The match was made in heaven, with both stars praising each other effusively and Kate favorably comparing the Duke to her former leading men, Spencer Tracy and Humphrey Bogart. Alas, the film itself is much ado about nothing. Shot on a skimpy budget with a sparse, largely uninteresting supporting cast, the flabby screenplay hardly does justice to its two stars. Director Stuart Millar also proves to be little more than serviceable in handling the action. At least two of the film's major sequences are blatantly recycled from *The African Queen* (1951) and— of all movies—*From Russia With Love* (1963)! (For example, Hepburn heads down the rolling rapids with Duke, just the way she did with Bogart 24 years earlier. And, like James Bond, Wayne dumps explosives into the river behind him, then fires his gun at them, causing them to explode and thus slowing down the enemy.)

Fortunately, the stars show enough charisma to ensure that much of *Rooster Cogburn* is indeed delightful. As *Variety* pointed out, unlike most contemporary movies, which rush through the dialogue to get to the action, this one is quite the opposite. Wayne hams it up mercilessly, but his interaction with the Great Kate gives the movie several memorable moments. Pity the fact that they never costarred in a vehicle worthy of their talents.

Did You Know . . . ?

★ It was rumored that Wayne and Hepburn would team again in another *True Grit* sequel titled *Someday*. The weak box office response to *Rooster Cogburn* probably prevented the project from being realized.

Rooster Heartburn

Don't let the title scare you away. This zesty, quick, and easy dish can be made with mild salsa to lessen its bite!

INGREDIENTS:
1 *12-ounce jar salsa mix*
1 *pound chicken fillets*
Spanish rice mix

EQUIPMENT:
2-quart casserole dish
Medium saucepan

Place a layer of the chicken on the bottom of a casserole dish in a 375° F. oven for 30 minutes or until golden brown. While the chicken is browning, prepare the Spanish rice in a saucepan according to package directions. Dump half a jar of salsa on top of the chicken, then add a layer of rice, and then the rest of the salsa. Bake for an additional 10 to 15 minutes. Serves 2 to 4.

Fowls of the Saddle

(*Pals of the Saddle,* 1938)

An easy chicken dish, straight from the mine to your table.

INGREDIENTS:
- 1 pound chicken fillets
- 1 2.8-ounce can french fried onions

3–4 *slices Swiss cheese*

EQUIPMENT:
2 quart casserole dish

Place chicken in the casserole dish and brown in a 375° F. oven for one half-hour. Cover the chicken with a layer of fried onions, then top with a layer of cheese. Bake until cheese is melted (about 5 minutes)—don't burn it! Serves 2 to 4.

Lady From Louisiana's Cajun Chicken

(*Lady From Louisiana,* 1941)

That high-spirited Southern belle sho-nuff makes a high-spirited chicken dish! Thanks to "Southern" Sarah Hamilton.

INGREDIENTS:
- 1 package of chicken (about 2 pounds)
- 2½ tablespoons paprika
- 2 tablespoons garlic powder
- 1 tablespoon salt
- 1 tablespoon onion powder
- 1 tablespoon ground thyme
- 1 tablespoon ground red pepper

EQUIPMENT:
Small container for mixed spices
Large grill or frying pan

Mix all the dry ingredients together and set them aside in the container. Moisten the chicken and sprinkle both sides with the spices, then press the spices into the skin with your fingers. On a grill or in a frying pan, cook until the chicken is tender, about 7 minutes on each side over medium heat. Cook longer if the chicken has bones. Serves 4.

"Like I told you, it takes a while for the chicken to simmer!"

Flame of the Bar-B-Q Coast

(*Flame of the Barbary Coast,* 1945)

A homemade barbecue chicken dish that requires no barbecuing, served at El Dorado and other fine gambling establishments. Thanks for this recipe to "Lucky" Paul Swindells.

INGREDIENTS:
- 1 *large family package (about 4 to 6 pounds) of chicken parts (legs, wings, thighs)*
- 1 *cup ketchup*
- 1 *cup dark brown sugar*

- 1 *cup white vinegar*
- 1 *cup onions, finely chopped*
- 1 *teaspoon dry mustard*

EQUIPMENT:
Stock pot with lid

In the stock pot, add all the ingredients, mixing well. Let simmer, covered, stirring occasionally, for 1½ hours, or until the chicken falls off the bone. Serves 6 to 8.

The Man From Monterey Jack

(*The Man From Monterey,* 1933)

A delicious chicken dish made with that special kind of cheese.

INGREDIENTS:
2 tablespoons salted butter
½ pound mushrooms
1 garlic clove
1 cup chopped onion
2 tablespoons all-purpose flour
1 cup half-and-half
   Salt and pepper to taste
6 chicken fillets (about
   1½ pounds of meat)
   Paprika (dash)
   Dried chopped parsley

6 slices (about 6 ounces)
   ham
6 slices Monterey Jack
   cheese
   Milk for basting (about
   4 ounces)

EQUIPMENT:
Cutting board
Medium skillet
Large baking pan

Slice the mushrooms, mince the garlic, and set aside. In the skillet, melt the butter and in it saute the mushrooms, garlic, and onion, stirring and tossing for 5 minutes over medium flame. Sprinkle on flour and saute another minute, stirring well. Gradually stir in the half-and-half and continue to cook until the sauce thickens (about six minutes over low flame). Add salt and pepper to taste.

Sprinkle the chicken generously with paprika and chopped parsley, and tightly wrap a slice of ham around each piece. Place the chicken rolls in the baking pan and top each with a slice of cheese.

Pour on the sauce and bake for 1½ hours at 350° F., basting with milk as necessary. Serves 4 to 6.

Central Airport

(*Central Airport,* 1933)

A hearty chicken casserole, coming in for a landing.

INGREDIENTS:
1 *whole chicken fryer (about*
   4 pounds)
1 *stick butter (salted)*
1 *10-ounce can cream of*
   mushroom soup
1 *10-ounce can cream of*
   chicken soup

1 *8-ounce package corn*
   bread stuffing mix
   Shortening

EQUIPMENT:
Large pot
Medium saucepan
Large casserole dish

Cut up the chicken, then boil the pieces (adding no salt to the water) approximately 30 to 40 minutes or until juice runs clear. Remove from the water and allow the chicken to cool. Tear the meat off the bones and set it aside. Save the broth.

In the saucepan, melt the butter and add the stuffing. Stir it up until all the butter has been absorbed and it's warm.

Grease the bottom of the casserole dish with shortening. Put a layer of stuffing in the dish, then add some chicken, and then the can of mushroom soup, spread evenly over the chicken. Fill the empty soup can with broth from the cooked chicken, and pour it into the casserole dish. Begin the steps again: a layer of stuffing, the rest of the chicken meat, the can of cream of chicken soup, and an empty can filled with chicken broth. Lastly, top with remaining stuffing.

Bake at 350° F. until brown, 45 minutes to an hour. Let sit for 15 minutes, then serve. Serves 2 to 4.

Shadow of the Eagle

(*Shadow of the Eagle*, 1932)

The duck is but a shadow of the eagle, but this duck with orange glaze will be a legend in its dinnertime!

INGREDIENTS:
- 1 4- to 5-pound duckling
- 6 orange slices
- ⅓ cup dark brown sugar, firmly packed
- ⅓ cup white sugar
- 1 tablespoon corn starch
- 1 tablespoon dried grated orange rind

- 1 cup orange juice
- ¼ teaspoon salt
-    Salt and Pepper to taste

EQUIPMENT:
Large roaster pot
Medium saucepan

Season the skin of the bird with salt and pepper. Fasten the neck skin to the back, close the body opening, and tie the legs with cooking twine. Roast in a 325° F. oven for 3 hours, or until well browned and tender.

While the duck is cooking, prepare the glaze: In the saucepan, combine the sugars and corn starch, add the grated orange, orange juice, and dash or two of salt. Stir over low heat until the sugars dissolve, then simmer until the sauce thickens (about 6 minutes).

When the duck is done roasting, remove it from the oven and halve it lengthwise, then crosswise. Arrange it on a platter with orange slice garnish. Pour some glaze over the bird, then, while serving, pass the rest of the sauce around. Serves 2 to 4.

The Conqueror

Cast: John Wayne, Susan Hayward, Pedro Armendariz,
   Agnes Moorehead
Director: Dick Powell
Released by RKO Radio Pictures (1956)

Y er Beeootiful in yer wrath!" With those words, John Wayne made screen history in a way he would have preferred not to. For Duke was cast as Genghis Khan when he growled this sultry mating call to his captive woman, Susan Hayward. Whatever possessed Wayne to take on this role may never be known, but lovers of bad movies will be eternally grateful for his lapse in judgment. The big-budget production presents Wayne with a droopy mustache, slanted eyes, and a toupee so cheesy it makes him resemble a cross between Ringo Starr and Moe Howard of the Three Stooges.

The film was financed by Howard Hughes, who owned RKO at the time. Hughes provided a sizable budget for actor and director Dick Powell to create some large-scale action sequences in the Utah desert. The battle sequences are indeed impressive, but the historical aspects of the story are on par with the "tits and togas" spectacles of the 1950s. Reaction to the movie was predictable: it became the laugh riot of the year (although it did gross a tidy sum on the basis of Wayne's box office pull). Hughes became enraged and withdrew the film from release, and it remained unseen until the reclusive billionaire's death. (Perhaps *The Conqueror* provided the reason for Hughes ultimately becoming a virtual hermit. After all, would *you* show your face again after you spent a fortune to cast John Wayne as Genghis Khan?)

Did You Know . . . ?

★ Wayne's role in *The Conqueror* inspired the title of a book about the worst casting decisions in screen history: *Starring John Wayne as Genghis Khan* (Citadel Press).

★ A tragic aftermath occurred in the wake of filming. A disproportionate number of the cast and crew eventually developed fatal cancer—probably due to the fact that the Utah location had previously been a test site for nuclear bombs.

The Conqueror's Stir Fry

Genghis would have flipped his hair hat for this delicious chicken dish.

INGREDIENTS:
- 2 *pounds chicken fillets*
- 1 *egg white*
- 1 *teaspoon corn starch*
- 1 *teaspoon soy sauce*
- ½ *teaspoon salt*
- 3 *medium zucchini*
- 2 *tablespoons corn starch*
- 2 *tablespoons cold water*
- 3 *tablespoons vegetable oil*
- 1 *medium fresh onion, thinly sliced*
- 2 *large garlic cloves, finely chopped*
- 1 *teaspoon ginger root, finely chopped*
- 8 *ounces mushrooms, sliced*
- ½ *cup chicken broth*
- 2 *tablespoons soy sauce*

EQUIPMENT:
Medium bowl
Small bowl
12-inch skillet or wok

Cut the chicken into strips, approximately one inch by two inches. Mix the egg white, 1 teaspoon of corn starch, 1 teaspoon of soy sauce, and salt in a bowl. Add the chicken, stir, cover, and refrigerate for 20 minutes.

Cut the zucchini lengthwise in half, then cut each half diagonally into ¼-inch slices. Mix 2 tablespoons of corn starch with the water. Set aside.

Heat the oil in the skillet or wok over high heat until hot. Add the chicken. Cook and stir until the chicken turns white, about 3 minutes. Remove the chicken from the skillet. Slice the onion thin, finely chop the garlic, and add both, along with the gingerroot to the skillet. Cook and stir until the garlic is brown. Add the zucchini and mushrooms, and cook while stirring for 2 minutes. Stir the chicken back in, adding chicken broth and 2 tablespoons of soy sauce. Heat to boiling. Stir in the corn starch mixture. Boil and stir, about 1 minute. Makes 6 servings.

Fowl in the Saddle

(*Tall in the Saddle,* 1944)

This fowl has been saddled with a delicious cranberry dressing. With thanks to the saddle-sore Judy Hamilton.

INGREDIENTS:
- 4 Cornish game hens (approx. 1½ pounds each)
- 4 cups of your favorite prepared stuffing
- ⅔ cup chopped cranberries Canola cooking oil
- ½ teaspoon minced onion
- ½ teaspoon garlic powder
- ½ teaspoon salt
- ½ teaspoon pepper

EQUIPMENT:
Medium saucepan
Large bowl
2-quart casserole dish or baking pan
Foil

Remove the giblets from the birds, then rinse inside and out with luke-warm water. Prepare the stuffing in the saucepan according to the directions on the box. Mix the cranberries and stuffing in a large bowl. Stuff each hen with approximately 1 cup of stuffing each.

Place the hens on a dish or tray and rub them with oil. Sprinkle the skins with the salt, pepper, onion, and garlic. Rub the seasonings into the skin.

Cover the tray loosely with aluminum foil. Cook in a 375° F. oven for 1½ hours (remove foil for the last half hour).

Baker of Hen

(*Maker of Men,* 1931)

Herb chicken that your team will love.

INGREDIENTS:
 3 pounds chicken pieces
 ½ cup salted butter
 5 tablespoons all-purpose flour
 1 teaspoon salt
 ¼ teaspoon pepper
 1 teaspoon ground dried thyme
 1 teaspoon dried rosemary

 2½ cups milk
 2½ tablespoons chopped fresh parsley
 1½ tablespoons chopped fresh chives

EQUIPMENT:
Large frying pan
Large casserole dish

Melt 2 tablespoons of butter in the pan. Brown the chicken on all sides over medium flame. Remove to the casserole dish.

Melt the remaining butter in the same pan. Blend in the flour, salt, pepper, thyme, and rosemary. Gradually add milk, stirring constantly. Add parsley and chives, and cook until thickened (about 4 to 6 minutes on low flame). Pour the mixture over the chicken and bake, uncovered, in a 350° F. oven for 1 hour, or until the chicken is tender.

Somewhere in Stroganoff

(*Somewhere in Sonora,* 1933)

All the gang will love this easy beef stroganoff.

INGREDIENTS:
1 *pound beef round*
1 *12-ounce can mushrooms*
1 *8-ounce can mushroom gravy*
1 *12-ounce bag egg noodles*

Canola oil

EQUIPMENT:
Large saucepan
2 large pots

Cut up the beef into bite-size pieces. Put in a saucepan that's been coated with a little cooking oil. Cook on medium heat. While meat is cooking, boil the noodles until fully cooked, drain, and put back in the pot.

After the meat is fully cooked, throw in mushrooms and gravy. Lower the heat and simmer for 10 minutes. Bring noodles to a boil and cook for 10 minutes. Serve meat over the noodles. Serves 2 to 4.

Lucky Texan Burger

(*Lucky Texan,* 1934)

A zesty treat that'll satisfy any cowpoke.

INGREDIENTS:
1 *pound lean ground beef*
⅓ *cup hot salsa mix*
¼ *cup Italian bread crumbs*

EQUIPMENT:
Medium mixing bowl
Medium grill or frying pan

Drain the juice from the salsa mix. Knead the salsa and bread crumbs into the ground beef until thoroughly mixed. Grill or fry just the way you like 'em.

Add a raw onion slice and your favorite condiments. For a zesty treat, melt a thin slice of Velveeta jalapeño cheese while the burger is still grilling.

You can control the spiciness of your burger—we suggest starting with hot salsa, since most of the "heat" gets grilled off.

Makes about 4 burgers.

The Fighting CBs

(*The Fighting Seabees,* 1944)

A unique take on an all-American favorite.

INGREDIENTS:
 2 *cups canned tomato sauce*
1½ *pounds lean ground beef*
 1 *large egg*
 2 *garlic cloves*
1½ *teaspoons seasoned salt*
 ¼ *teaspoon pepper*
 1 *tablespoon salted butter*
 6 *slices sharp Cheddar cheese*

EQUIPMENT:
Small pot
Small bowl
Large bowl
Large frying pan or grill
Serving bowl

Heat the sauce in a small pot and keep hot.

Beat the egg in a small bowl and crush the garlic, then mix with the beef, seasoned salt, and pepper. Shape into 6 patties. Brown on both sides in a buttered skillet or on a grill over medium flame (about 5 minutes). Cover each patty with a cheese slice and cook 3 minutes longer, or until cheese is melted.

Pour the sauce into a serving dish and arrange the cheeseburgers in the sauce. Serves 4 to 6.

Pittsburgher

(Pittsburgh, 1942)

From the steel mills to your kitchen!

INGREDIENTS:
1 *pound lean ground beef*
½ *cup minced onions*
2 *tablespoons butter*
1 *teaspoon salt*
  Dash pepper

Dash ground thyme
½ *cup red wine*

EQUIPMENT:
Medium frying pan
Mixing bowl

For every pound of ground beef, saute ½ cup of minced onions in 2 tablespoons of butter until the onions are tender. Mix the onions with the raw beef, 1 teaspoon of salt, a pinch of pepper, and a pinch of thyme.

Pan fry the burgers in equal parts of butter and oil (about 1½ teaspoons each). When the patties are medium rare, remove them to a hot platter and deglaze the pan with ½ cup of red wine. Be sure to scrape up all the pan juices and brownings and heat the wine so it reduces at least by half. Remove from the heat, add a teaspoon of soft butter, stir briefly, and pour it over the hamburgers. Serve on toasted buns. Makes 2 to 4 servings.

King of the Tacos

(*King of the Pecos,* 1936)

These classic tacos reign supreme. With thanks to "Pecos" Paul Swindells.

INGREDIENTS:
1 *pound lean ground beef*
3 *garlic cloves*
1 *tablespoon paprika*
½ *tablespoon dried oregano*
½ *teaspoon ground cumin*
1 *medium onion*
½ *head lettuce*
1 *12-ounce package shredded Cheddar cheese*

1 *large tomato*
1 *medium jalapeño pepper*
¼ *cup green salsa*
3 *tablespoons water*
  Dash Red Hot sauce
  Taco shells

EQUIPMENT:
Small frying pan
Bowls for toppings

Crush the garlic, chop half of the onion and pepper and set aside. Chop the tomato and onion and shred the lettuce, and set these toppings aside into individual bowls. Brown the beef over high heat, then drain well. Add water, salsa, and onion. Lower the heat and let simmer for about 5 minutes, then add the garlic, paprika, oregano, cumin, pepper, and hot sauce, and continue to simmer, about 10 minutes.

Heat the taco shells in a warm oven for about 10 minutes—don't burn them! Fill the shells with the meat mixture, then add the toppings to taste. Serves 2 to 4.

The Meat Loaf From Utah

(The Man From Utah, 1934)

Everybody at the rodeo will be asking: What exactly is that meat loaf made from? Thanks for the recipe to "Sheriff" Judy Hamilton.

INGREDIENTS:
¾ cup bread crumbs
2 large eggs
½ cup tomato juice or sauce
2 tablespoons parsley
½ teaspoon oregano
¼ teaspoon salt
¼ teaspoon pepper
1 garlic clove
2 pounds lean ground beef

6 thin slices mozzarella
   cheese
½ pound boiled ham (4–6
   thin slices)
Dash paprika

EQUIPMENT:
Mixing bowl
Wax paper or aluminum foil
13 × 9-inch pan

Beat the eggs in the bowl, then combine the eggs with the tomato juice. Stir in the bread crumbs and all spices except the paprika. Then add the beef and mix well. On a piece of wax paper or foil, form meat into an approximately 10 × 8-inch rectangle. Arrange the ham slices in a layer on top of the meat, leaving a small margin around the edges. Then arrange a layer of cheese on top of the ham, setting aside one slice.

Roll the meat jelly-roll style, then smooth it out so you don't see the seam or the ends. Arrange the loaf seam-side down in the baking pan. Sprinkle paprika on top. Bake in a 350° F. oven for 1¼ hours. Remove from the oven, arrange the last piece of cheese on top, and cook another 1 to 2 minutes, until the cheese melts.

Note: The meat may look raw when you slice it—that's an illusion created by the ribbon of ham.

Three-Pound Texas Steer

(*Three Texas Steers*, 1939)

A steak marinade that will have everyone saddling up to the table.

INGREDIENTS:
- 1 2–3 pound steak
- 2–3 tablespoons soy sauce
- 1 tablespoon salad oil
- 1 tablespoon tomato paste
- 1 teaspoon salt
- ½ teaspoon pepper
- ½ teaspoon dried oregano
- 2 garlic cloves

EQUIPMENT:
Medium bowl
Large Ziploc bag

Mix all the ingredients in bowl and spread them over the meat. Put everything into a Ziploc bag and close securely. Refrigerate for at least 5 hours—the flavor improves with longer storage.

Remove from the refrigerator and grill to perfection! Serves 4 to 6.

Chisum

Cast: John Wayne, Forrest Tucker, Christopher George,
Pamela McMyler, Geoffrey Deuel, Ben Johnson, Bruce Cabot
Director: Andrew V. McLaglen
Released by Warner Bros (1970)

*C*hisum was the first John Wayne film to be released following the actor's triumphant Oscar win for *True Grit*. Its story is loosely based on the infamous Lincoln County Wars, and Wayne was portraying a real-life character, albeit with a good deal of artistic license. Wayne's Chisum is the benevolent cattle king reigning over a large empire. He comes into conflict over land rights with another baron played by Forrest Tucker. The two strong-willed adversaries enlist their own private armies to do battle. Naturally, it is the Tucker character who plays dirty and causes peace-loving Wayne to renounce pacifism and "do what I'd have done twenty years ago!" This entails leading his men in a massive assault on Tucker's forces in a terrific climax.

Chisum benefits from a sterling cast, with Tucker proving to be everything that a great movie villain requires. He is charming, witty, cultured—and utterly ruthless. His scenes with Wayne ring with conviction and tension, and one wishes they had made more films together.

Chisum is also one of the best of the Duke's collaborations with director Andrew V. McLaglen, a man with a checkered list of credentials. His work with the Duke includes the banal (*Cahill: U.S. Marshall,* 1973), the corny (*The Undefeated,* 1969), and the ludicrous (*Hellfighters,* 1968), although he also directed the rollicking *McLintock!* (1963) and several excellent non-Wayne vehicles, including *The Wild Geese* (1978) and *The Sea Wolves* (1980).

Did You Know . . . ?

★ President Nixon publicly praised *Chisum* as one of his favorite films. Democrats, however, argued that the movie inspired him to launch covert invasions into Cambodia!

Chisum's Chili

A staple almost every night on John Chisum's table, either as a side or an entrée. Thanks to Paul "the Kid" Swindells.

INGREDIENTS:
1½ *pounds lean ground beef*
 2 *tablespoons olive oil*
1½ *large sweet onions*
 2 *jalapeño peppers*
 1 *28-ounce can crushed tomatoes*
 4 *heaping tablespoons chili powder (don't be shy!)*
 6 *tablespoons taco seasoning*

4 *teaspoons ground cumin*
4 *tablespoons ground oregano*
1 *teaspoon salt*
4 *garlic cloves*

EQUIPMENT:
2 small bowls
Crock pot

Finely chop the onions and peppers and set aside. Crush the garlic and set it aside. Brown the ground beef in a large skillet and drain. Add the browned beef and crushed tomatoes to the crock pot. Cook over high heat for 15 minutes, then stir in all the remaining ingredients. Cook on low heat for 4 hours, stirring occasionally. Serves 4 to 6.

Words and Meatball

(*Words and Music,* 1929)

The words you will hear when you serve these Swedish meatballs will be something like "Yum yum!," "Delicious," and (dare we say), "Can I have the recipe?"

INGREDIENTS:
- ¼ cup bread crumbs
- ⅓ cup milk
- 1 pound lean ground beef
- 1 small onion
- 1 teaspoon salt
- ¼ teaspoon pepper
-   Dash ground allspice
-   Dash ground cloves
-   Dash ground nutmeg
- 1 large egg
- 3 tablespoons shortening
- 2 tablespoons all-purpose flour
- 1 cup water
- ½ cup milk

EQUIPMENT:
Small bowl
Medium bowl
Large bowl
Large saucepan or frying pan

Soak the bread crumbs in ⅓ cup of milk in the medium bowl. Finely chop the onion in the large bowl, then mix it with the meat and all seasonings. Slightly beat the egg in the small bowl, then add it and the soaked bread crumbs to the meat mixture. Mix well.

Shape into small meatballs, brown in the pan over medium flame. Pour off excess fat. Sprinkle the meatballs with flour and roll around. Add water. Cover and simmer, about 20 minutes. Add ½ cup of milk and simmer again until hot over low flame. Makes 4 servings.

The Long Voyage Home

Cast: John Wayne, Thomas Mitchell, Ian Hunter, Barry Fitzgerald,
   Wilfrid Lawson, Mildred Natwick, John Qualen
Director: John Ford
Released by United Artists (1940)

One of the more unusual of John Wayne's films, *The Long Voyage Home,* was an offbeat, ambitious attempt by director John Ford to make a mainstream success of what was primarily an art house movie. Based on several plays by Eugene O'Neill, the story centers on the lives of a motley group of seaman aboard a rundown steamer. The men are crude, rude, and often vulgar, but display an admirable sense of camaraderie and loyalty to each other and their superiors. Wayne was Ford's unorthodox choice for the lead role of Ole Olsen, a young and naïve sailor who is watched over and protected by his more seasoned shipmates. The film's leisurely pace traces the crew through various ports of call and allows the audience to get to know each character intimately before the final, tragic conclusion.

Wayne was nervous playing a character with a Swedish accent. Despite taking diction lessons from a Danish actress (who was close enough to Swedish to suit crotchety director Ford), Duke never felt his performance was very persuasive. Critics disagreed. Wayne received high marks, as did his fellow cast members. The film was nominated for several Oscars, including Best Picture. Commercial success did not follow, however. The movie was far too somber and talky for everyday audiences, and its grosses were weak. Still, in later years, both Wayne and Ford would live to see the movie regarded as a cult classic. For the Duke, it proved he could be accepted in an unconventional role. Yet he was still uneasy about his performance and would refrain from playing a character with an accent for the rest of his career.

Did You Know . . . ?

★ To publicize the film as a work of art, the producer hired several great American painters, including Grant Wood, to render their impressions of the film on canvas. The resulting paintings toured the United States as part of an effort to promote interest in the art world and the cinema.

The Long Voyage Home

Tragically, this tuna never made it's voyage home, but wound up in this casserole instead.

INGREDIENTS:
- 1 tablespoon butter or margarine
- ¼ cup chopped onion
- ¼ cup chopped green pepper
- 1 4-ounce can mushrooms
- 2 6½-ounce cans tuna, drained and flaked
- 1 medium tomato
- 1 tablespoon lemon juice extract
- ¼ teaspoon salt
- ⅛ teaspoon pepper
- ¾ cup mayonnaise
- ½ pound elbow macaroni or ziti
- ½ cup shredded Cheddar cheese

EQUIPMENT:

Large pot	*Large bowl*
Small bowl	*Medium pot*
Small skillet	*2-quart casserole*

Cook the noodles until tender in a pot of boiling water. Peel, chop, and drain the tomato, and set it aside. Melt the butter in the skillet. Over medium heat, saute the onion, green pepper, and mushrooms, stirring often until tender. Stir together the tuna, tomato, lemon, salt, pepper, and mayonnaise. Add the cooked noodles and sauteed ingredients, and mix well. Pour into greased casserole dish. Top with cheese. Bake uncovered in a 400° F. oven for 20 minutes, or until heated and the cheese has melted. Serves 4 to 6.

Donovan's Reef

Cast: John Wayne, Lee Marvin, Elizabeth Allen, Jack Warden,
Cesar Romero, Dorothy Lamour
Director: John Ford
Released by Paramount Pictures (1963)

It is rather sad to realize that the last John Wayne collaboration with his legendary mentor John Ford was this glorified home movie shot on location in Hawaii. Wayne and Lee Marvin star as wartime antagonists who meet on the island paradise annually to continue their good-natured feud. Nothing of any consequence happens in the film, though the chemistry between Wayne and Marvin is terrific. Apparently, Ford (who was in declining health) and his stock company simply wanted to enjoy a vacation in the sun. The paper-thin *Donovan's Reef* was the result of that excursion. The scenery is wonderful and there are some good musical interludes, but considering that Ford would continue to make movies for the next two years (*Cheyenne Autumn,* 1964, *7 Women,* 1966), it is all the more depressing to realize that the best he and the Duke could come up with for their final joint venture was this lightweight confection.

Did You Know . . . ?

★ *Donovan's Reef* marked the third and final time the Duke and Lee Marvin costarred. They previously appeared together in *The Man Who Shot Liberty Valance* (1962) and *The Comancheros* (1961).

Donovan's Reef Salmon Steak

A tasty teriyaki salmon steak, grilled to perfection.

INGREDIENTS:
- 4 ¾- to 1-inch thick salmon steaks (approx. 8–10 ounces each)
- ¼ cup soy sauce
- 2 tablespoons dark brown sugar
- 2 teaspoons finely chopped garlic
- 2 teaspoons fresh lemon juice
- ½ teaspoon sesame oil
- ¼ teaspoon salt

EQUIPMENT:
Large, shallow glass dish
Grilling brush

Combine all the ingredients for the sauce in a glass dish. Add the salmon steaks and turn to coat. Let them stand in the sauce for 20 minutes.

Arrange the salmon on a grill. Grill over medium-hot coals, brushing frequently with the sauce, for 4 to 5 minutes per side, until cooked through. (Appearance of the fish will be opaque.)

Three Codfathers

(*Three Godfathers,* 1948)

A trio of delicious cod recipes. Cook 'em just the way you like 'em!

BAKED COD

INGREDIENTS:
1½ pounds cod fillets
  1 teaspoon ground sage
  ½ cup grated Swiss cheese
  1 cup sour cream

Salt and pepper to taste

EQUIPMENT:
2-quart glass baking dish

Wash and dry the codfish. Sprinkle both sides of the fillets with salt, pepper, and sage. Place them in a greased, shallow baking dish. Sprinkle the cheese on top and cover with sour cream. Bake for 25 minutes at 350° F. Serves 2 to 4.

BROILED COD

INGREDIENTS:
  1 pound frozen cod fillets
2½ tablespoons salted butter
  1 teaspoon dried minced
    parsley
  2 teaspoons dried chopped
    onion

½ cup milk
  Salt and pepper to taste

EQUIPMENT:
baking pan 8 × 8 × 2 inches

Remove the cod from the freezer and, when partially thawed, cut into quarters. Grease the pan and place the cod in the pan. Melt the butter and brush it onto the cod. Sprinkle on salt and pepper. Pour the milk around the fillets and cover with onion and parsley. Broil for about 15 minutes, until nicely browned, basting occasionally. Serves 2 to 4.

COD FISH CAKES

INGREDIENTS:

1 pound cod fillets (fresh or frozen)
4–5 medium potatoes
1 medium onion
2 tablespoons fresh parsley
1 large egg
Sprinkling of seasoning salt
½ teaspoon salt
¼ teaspoon pepper
Bread crumbs

Canola oil
Lemon or tartar sauce (optional)

EQUIPMENT:
Small bowl
Medium pot
Large pot
Large frying pan

Grate the onion, chop the parsley, beat the egg, and set all aside. Place the fillets in enough water to cover them, bring to boil, and cook five more minutes on high. Peel and boil the potatoes on high until tender (test with fork); drain and mash.

Drain and flake the cod fillets in the mixing bowl (use your fingers to remove any bones). Add slightly cooled mashed potatoes, the onions, parsley, beaten egg, salt, pepper, and seasoning salt. Mix well and form into patties. Coat the fish cakes with the bread crumbs. Fry in cooking oil over medium flame until brown on both sides. Drain and soak on paper towels. Serve with lemon sauce or tartar sauce. Serves 2 to 4.

Bluefish Steel

(*Blue Steel*, 1934)

A bluefish dish for outlaws and marshals alike.

INGREDIENTS:
3–5 pounds dressed bluefish
  1 tablespoon mayonnaise
  2 lemons
  1 medium onion
  2 tablespoons chopped fresh
    parsley

Paprika (about 1 teaspoon)
Salt and pepper to taste

EQUIPMENT:
2-quart glass baking dish
Foil

Preheat the oven to 500° F. Chop the onion and slice the lemons. Wash and dry the fish. Salt and pepper the fish, and coat with mayonnaise inside and out. Place the fish on foil in the baking pan. Arrange the lemon slices on top, and sprinkle on the onion and parsley. Dust with paprika. Turn the oven down to 400° F. Bake for 10 minutes per pound. Serves 6.

The Prawn Rider

(*The Dawn Rider*, 1935)

This spicy shrimp will bring the desperadoes to the dinner table.

INGREDIENTS:
  ½ large onion
  ½ cup chopped mushrooms
  2 tablespoons butter
  2 tablespoons flour
  1 cup mushroom broth
  1 cup water
  2 cups cooked and cleaned
    large shrimp
  ½ teaspoon salt

  ⅛ teaspoon black pepper
    Dash cayenne pepper
  ¼ teaspoon ground thyme
  1 bay leaf
  2 fresh pimentos

EQUIPMENT:
2 small bowls
Large saucepan

Chop the onion; saute it with the mushrooms in butter for 3 minutes over low flame. Stir in the flour. Add the mushroom broth and water and cook until thickened, stirring constantly. Chop the pimentos. Combine with all the remaining ingredients in the saucepan. Cook for 5 minutes. Serve with rice. Makes 2 to 4 servings.

Rainbow Trout Valley

(*Rainbow Valley*, 1935)

The valley was known as the home of the most delicious trout this side of the Pecos.

INGREDIENTS:
1 garlic clove
1 teaspoon ground thyme
¼ teaspoon black pepper
6 whole pan dressed trout
(about ¾ pound each)
6 bay leaves
4 tablespoons salted butter

Juice of 2 lemons
¼ cup finely minced fresh
parsley

EQUIPMENT:
Small bowl
Small saucepan
Large baking dish

Blend together the garlic, thyme, and pepper, and spread on the trout. Insert 1 whole bay leaf inside each fish. Grease a baking dish that is large enough to hold a single layer of fish. Melt the butter in the saucepan and pour over the fish. Bake 10 to 12 minutes in a 400° F. oven (flake with a fork to test). Sprinkle with lemon juice and parsley before serving. Serves 4 to 6.

Operation Pacific

(*Operation Pacific,* 1951)

Would you believe us if we told you that the U.S. submarine Thunderfish caught these jewels of the sea, and the chef whipped them together, much to the lieutenant commander's delight? We didn't think so.

INGREDIENTS:
- 1 1¼-pound lobster
- 3 ounces crabmeat
- 2 shrimps
- 1 ounce clarified butter
- 1 tablespoon shallots
- 2 ounces white wine

- 2 ounces raw butter (salted)
- 1 tablespoon chopped dried parsley
- Salt and pepper to taste

EQUIPMENT:
Large saucepan

Saute the shrimp in clarified butter until cooked (3 to 5 minutes on medium). Add the shallots, and saute 3 to 5 minutes until golden brown. Add crabmeat and meat from the lobster, and toss lightly. Add wine and raw butter, and toss lightly again. Season to taste, then simmer for 2 minutes. Add parsley and serve. Makes 1 to 2 servings.

The Broilers

(The Spoilers, 1942)

Upon his escape from jail, Roy sat down to enjoy these broiled scallops.

INGREDIENTS:
- 1 pound fresh scallops
- ¼ stick salted butter
- ¼ cup olive oil
- 2 garlic cloves
- 1 tablespoon lemon juice
- 1 ounce Sauterne or white wine
- 1 teaspoon dried parsley
- Paprika (about 1 teaspoon)

EQUIPMENT:
Cutting board
Medium saucepan
Large baking sheet

Chop the garlic. Saute the oil, butter, and garlic until lightly browned. Remove from the heat to cool a minute, then add the lemon, wine, and parsley.

Lay the scallops flat on a baking sheet. Pour all the ingredients over scallops. Sprinkle with paprika and broil for 2 minutes. Serves 2 to 4.

Meatless Frontier Lasagna

(*Lawless Frontier*, 1935)

Sometimes meat was hard to come by on the frontier. Here is a meatless lasagna that will satisfy every outlaw.

INGREDIENTS:
- 1 pound lasagna noodles
- 1 cup Fontina cheese, shredded
- 1 10-ounce package frozen spinach, thawed and well drained
- 1 cup fresh shredded carrots
- 1 cup fresh shredded zucchini
- 3 cups (24 ounces) part skim milk ricotta cheese
- 1 large egg
- 1 medium onion
- 1 tablespoon cooking oil
- 2 tablespoons all-purpose flour
- ¼ teaspoon ground nutmeg
- 1 cup vegetable or chicken broth
- ½ cup Parmesan cheese

EQUIPMENT:
Large pot
Foil
Medium bowl
13 × 9-inch baking dish
Medium pot

Cook the noodles until tender (about 8 to 10 minutes on high flame), then drain and lay them out flat on the foil. Combine Fontina cheese and the vegetables with 2½ cups of the ricotta cheese and the egg. Place a bottom layer of noodles in the baking dish. Spread with half of the cheese and vegetable mixture. Repeat the layers, ending with a layer of lasagna.

Chop the onion and saute in the oil until tender over medium flame. Add flour and nutmeg. Stir in the broth and remaining ricotta. Cook and stir until the mixture comes to a boil. Spoon over the lasagna. Sprinkle on Parmesan. Cover with foil and bake at 350° F. for 45 minutes. Uncover and broil for another 2 to 3 minutes, or until slightly browned. Serves 8.

SAGEBRUSH
SIDES

"Hey, boys! Save room for the Fort Apacheese and Rio Brocco."

Cast a Giant Shadow

Cast: Kirk Douglas, Senta Berger, Angie Dickinson, John Wayne,
Frank Sinatra, Yul Brynner
Director: Melville Shavelson
Released by United Artists (1966)

An offbeat and often underrated film, *Cast a Giant Shadow* was a box office flop upon its release in 1966. The movie tells the story of Mickey Marcus, a career American army officer who reluctantly agreed to train Israel's ragtag army on the eve of its independence. Knowing the new nation would be invaded by its Arab neighbors, Marcus rose to the challenge and created a formidable fighting force, which won against seemingly insurmountable odds. Tragically, Marcus was accidentally killed by one of his own men.

Director and producer Melville Shavelson could not get studio funding for the film because it was "too Jewish" to appeal to mainstream audiences. Shavelson was shocked when Duke Wayne agreed to help produce the movie and to take a supporting role opposite star Kirk Douglas, who played Marcus. Wayne admired Shavelson for his passion for the story and felt there was something inherently American about Israel's fight for independence. With Wayne onboard, Shavelson succeeded in getting United Artists to back the film. He also persuaded Yul Brynner and Frank Sinatra to make memorable cameo appearances.

Despite its many qualities, *Cast a Giant Shadow* was neither a critical nor a financial success, possibly due to a confusing marketing campaign which tried to disguise the movie as a World War II epic. Nonetheless, this is an ambitious and engrossing movie well worth a look.

Did You Know . . . ?

★ Melville Shavelson wrote a hilarious book about his frustration in bringing this film to the screen. Its title? *How to Make a Jewish Movie.*

Quiche a Giant Shadow

Even real men like General Randolph have been known to eat this delicious quiche. But they'll probably never admit it!

INGREDIENTS:
12 slices bacon
 1 cup (4 ounces) shredded
     natural Swiss cheese
 ⅓ cup chopped onion
 2 cups milk
 1 cup Bisquick baking mix
 4 large eggs

¼ teaspoon salt
⅛ teaspoon pepper

EQUIPMENT:
10-inch pie plate
Medium bowl
Small frying pan
Electric mixer

Fry the bacon and crumble it into pieces. Preheat the oven to 400° F. Lightly grease the pie plate and sprinkle in the bacon, cheese, and onion. In the bowl, beat the milk, Bisquick, eggs, salt, and pepper until smooth, using the mixer (about 1 minute). Pour the mixture into the pie plate.

Bake for 35 minutes or until the top is golden brown and a knife inserted halfway between the center and the edge comes out clean. Let stand 5 minutes before cutting. Serves 4.

Hellfighters

Cast: John Wayne, Katharine Ross, Jim Hutton, Vera Miles,
Bruce Cabot
Director: Andrew V. McLaglen
Released by Universal Pictures (1968)

Best described as a cross between *The Towering Inferno* and *As the World Turns, Hellfighters* is a film only a hopeless romantic or a pyromaniac could love. If oil and water don't mix, neither do the attempts by the scriptwriters to mingle love scenes with blazing infernos.

Hellfighters is thoroughly acceptable on a B-movie level when it sticks to the often impressive action sequences. It's the frequent detours into domestic squabbling between Duke Wayne and onscreen spouse Vera Miles that derail the story completely. Equally absurd are the attempts to appeal to a young audience via generation gap problems faced by "youngsters" Katharine Ross and Jim Hutton (who wear more polyester than can be found in any twenty issues of *Modern Maturity* magazine—they best not get near a flame, or *they* could be scorched, too!). These sequences are so out of touch with the real world that it makes *The Brady Bunch* seem like slice-of-life drama.

If you're planning on preparing our *Hellfighters*-inspired recipe, make sure the dish isn't as half-baked as the film.

Did You Know . . . ?

★ The story of *Hellfighters* was loosely based on the real-life exploits of Red Adair, who pioneered effective oil fighting techniques. Adair also served as technical advisor on the film.

Hellfritters

Corn fritters, that is, and you'll catch hell if you don't clean your plate.

INGREDIENTS:
1 cup corn (fresh, cut from the
   cob, and coarsely chopped;
   or frozen kernels, thawed
   and drained)
2 large eggs
¼ cup all-purpose flour
4 Saltine crackers
½ teaspoon baking powder

1 teaspoon sugar
¼ teaspoon salt
   Pinch cayenne pepper
   Pinch ground nutmeg

EQUIPMENT:
2 medium bowls
Griddle

Beat the eggs well. Add the corn and set aside. Grind up the Saltines until fine. Mix together all dry ingredients well, and fold into the corn mixture. Melt a pat of butter onto a hot griddle. Cook the corn batter in spoonfuls on griddle (about 6 to 8 minutes on low). Makes 4 servings.

Rio Grande

Cast: John Wayne, Maureen O'Hara, Ben Johnson, Claude Jarman, Jr., Harry Carey, Jr., Chill Wills, Victor McLaglen
Director: John Ford
Released by Republic Pictures (1950)

Rio Grande marked the last film in director John Ford's fabled "Cavalry Trilogy." For many critics it was also the least ambitious of the trio (which included *Fort Apache,* 1948, and *She Wore a Yellow Ribbon,* 1949) The movie is so leisurely paced that at times it appears as though Ford is guilty of padding the action with long musical interludes and dialogue which, although entertaining, are not especially relevant to the story. Nevertheless, the movie has much to recommend it, including the Duke's first teaming with Maureen O'Hara (they would ultimately make five films together).

Wayne plays a hard-bitten, no-nonsense cavalry commander who is frustrated by not being able to pursue Apache war parties across the border into Mexico. In true Duke Wayne style, he eventually ignores the red tape and leads a daring raid into Mexico to rescue a wagon load of children kidnapped by the Indians. The script was timely, as the film seemed to draw parallels to the ongoing conflict in Korea, in which the United Nations had forbidden troops from pursuing the Red Army into North Korea.

John Ford had little interest in doing this movie, but agreed to direct it on the condition that Republic would finance his long awaited dream project, *The Quiet Man.*

Did You Know . . . ?

★ Wayne's character is named Kirby Yorke. With the exception of the *e* at the end of Yorke, the name is identical to the person he portrayed in *Fort Apache.* Was John Ford telling us they are one and the same? If so, why spell the name differently? Film buffs have long debated Ford's intentions.

Rice-o Grande

A "dirty rice" dish enjoyed by all the soldiers in the fort.

INGREDIENTS:
 1 *small onion*
 1 *teaspoon garlic powder*
 ¼ *pound pork sausage*
 1 *cup converted rice*
 2½ *cups chicken broth*
 1 *tablespoon salted butter*

 1 *tablespoon ground thyme*
  Salt and pepper to taste

EQUIPMENT:
Cutting board
Small bowl
Large saucepan with lid

Dice the onion and set aside. Brown the sausage over medium flame, drain, and set it aside. Cook the onion and garlic in the butter until limp. Add the rice and seasonings and stir. Add the broth and sausage, bring to a hard boil, then reduce to a simmer. Cover and cook for 35 minutes without stirring or lifting the lid. Once the liquid is absorbed by the rice, the dish is ready. Serves 4.

On patrol for a tasty rice side dish.

War of the Wild Rice

(War of the Wildcats, 1943)

They'll be fighting over the last spoonfuls of this rice, much like Jim Gardner and Dan Somers fought over Cathy Allen.

INGREDIENTS:
 3 *cups cooked rice*
 ¼ *cup flour*
 1 *teaspoon salt*
 ½ *cup finely chopped fresh parsley*
 ⅓ *cup finely chopped onion*

2½ *cups light cream*
 Shortening

EQUIPMENT:
 Medium saucepan with lid
 Large bowl
 1½-quart shallow casserole dish

Boil 3 cups of instant rice in 3 cups of water. Remove from heat, stir, and cover for 5 minutes. Mix the rice, flour, salt, onion, and parsley. Spoon into a greased (with shortening) casserole dish. Pour light cream on the rice mixture. Bake at 350° F., uncovered, for 30 minutes or until set. Serves 6.

Reap the Wild Rice

(Reap the Wild Wind, 1942)

All who reap this wild rice will enjoy its flavorful advantages.

INGREDIENTS:
1½ *cups precooked wild rice*
 ½ *teaspoon salt*
 5 *tablespoons salted butter*
 1 *garlic clove, pressed*
 ½ *teaspoon dried chives*

4 *tablespoons grated Parmesan cheese*

EQUIPMENT:
 2 small saucepans

Follow cooking directions on the package for the rice. In the other saucepan, melt the butter, then add the pressed garlic and chives. Stir this into the fluffed rice. Sprinkle with cheese and stir lightly. Serves 4.

Fort Apache

Cast: Henry Fonda, John Wayne, Shirley Temple, Pedro Armendariz,
   John Agar, Ward Bond, Irene Rich, George O'Brien, Anna Lee
Director: John Ford
Released by RKO Radio Pictures (1948)

Although John Wayne had remained a top box office attraction since *Stagecoach* in 1939, he had primarily appeared in relatively undistinguished films ever since (exceptions being *The Long Voyage Home* [1940] and *They Were Expendable* [1945]). Not coincidentally, the three aforementioned classics were directed by John Ford. Although the crusty director was one of Wayne's most ardent admirers, even he had doubts about the Duke's acting ability. Therefore, when it came to casting *Fort Apache* in 1948, Ford hedged on casting Wayne in the leading role of prima donna cavalry Lt. Col. Owen Thursday, a Custer-like figure whose arrogance leads to the tragic massacre of his entire command. Instead, Ford opted for Henry Fonda, who was undeniably brilliant in the role. Still, Duke—relegated to what is very much a supporting role as Thursday's antagonist, Capt. Kirby York—managed to impress critics with his finest performance to date.

Fort Apache, the first film in Ford's "Cavalry Trilogy," which would include *She Wore A Yellow Ribbon* (1949) and *Rio Grande* (1950), is a masterful blend of humor, sentimentality, and thought-provoking drama.

Did You Know . . . ?

★ John Agar, who made his film debut in *Fort Apache,* was married to costar Shirley Temple.

Fort Apacheese

Macaroni and cheese that quells the hearty appetites of the entire Union army. With thanks to "Lt. Col." Judy Hamilton.

INGREDIENTS:
- 1 *pound elbow macaroni*
- 1 *teaspoon margarine or salted butter*
- 2 *tablespoons flour*
- ¾ *cup milk*
- 1½ *cups grated sharp Cheddar cheese*
- ¼ *cup Parmesan cheese*
- 1 *teaspoon paprika*
- *Bread crumbs (optional)*

EQUIPMENT:
Large boiling pot
Large saucepan
Large casserole dish

Cook the noodles 8 to 10 minutes until tender and set aside. Melt the butter in the saucepan. Stir in the flour, add milk, and stir until smooth. Stir in the cheese and keep mixing over low flame. Add the noodles to the cheese sauce mixture. Pour into the casserole dish. Sprinkle on paprika and optional bread crumbs. Bake for 20 to 30 minutes at 350° F. or until top is lightly browned. Serves 3 to 4.

The Lawless Noodles

(*The Lawless Nineties,* 1936)

These noodles go undercover in a delicious Alfredo-style cheese sauce.
Thanks to the always lawful Grace Murray.

INGREDIENTS:
- 6 *cups of cooked Pennsylvania Dutch medium noodles*
- 6 *tablespoons salted butter*
- ½ *pint heavy cream*
- 5 *ounces shredded Parmesan cheese*
- *Dash grated Romano cheese*

EQUIPMENT:
Large pot
Colander or strainer

Boil the noodles for 10 minutes, then drain and leave in the colander.
In the same pot, melt the butter, then add the cream and bring to a
boil. Put the noodles back in the pot. Stir in the cheeses and enjoy.
Serves 4 to 6.

Rio Bravo

Cast: John Wayne, Dean Martin, Ricky Nelson, Angie Dickinson,
Walter Brennan, Ward Bond, John Russell
Director: Howard Hawks
Released by Warner Bros. (1959)

The Duke reteamed with *Red River* director Howard Hawks for this western classic. Both Wayne and Hawks had been critical of *High Noon* (1952) because it depicted the inhabitants of the Old West mostly as cowards who let one courageous marshal defend them from a gang of thugs. In *Rio Bravo,* Wayne is Sheriff John T. Chance, a fearless lawman who is attempting to hold the brother of an influential land baron on charges of murder. Although up against a virtual army of hired assassins intent on springing his prisoner, Wayne is far from being the lone hero that *High Noon*'s Gary Cooper was. Wayne enlists a small band of odd-ball allies, including a drunken deputy (Dean Martin), a teenage gun-slinger (Ricky Nelson), a whore with a heart of gold (Angie Dickinson), and a grumpy but fearless old coot (Walter Brennan).

Rio Bravo represents Wayne and Hawks at their best. The leisurely screenplay is consistently engrossing, and each of the characters gets their moment to shine. Martin, who was all but dismissed as a boring straight man to Jerry Lewis, proved he had the ability to deliver a pow-

JOHN WAYNE | **DEAN MARTIN** | **RICKY NELSON** | **RIO BRAVO** | ANGIE DICKINSON · WALTER BRENNAN
WARD BOND · JOHN RUSSELL
TECHNICOLOR® from WARNER BROS.

erful dramatic performance, and Walter Brennan steals the show in a brilliant, often hilarious performance as Stumpy the stalwart crippled deputy. Indeed, the film was so good that Hawks himself could not stop himself from revisiting the property. Two of his future Wayne westerns— *El Dorado* and *Rio Lobo*—are virtual remakes of this film.

Did You Know . . . ?

★ *Rio Bravo* was remade in a contemporary setting by director John Carpenter as *Assault on Precinct 13* (1976).

Rio Brocco

Even Sheriff Chance likes this broccoli and cheese dish.

INGREDIENTS:
- 2 10-ounce boxes frozen chopped broccoli
- 1 small onion
- 1 cup rice
- ½ stick salted butter or margarine
- 2 10-ounce cans cream of chicken soup
- 1 cup sharp Cheddar cheese, shredded
- 1 soup can full of milk

EQUIPMENT:
Small bowl
Large saucepan

Chop the onion. Put the broccoli and rice in the pan. Add enough water to prevent sticking. Cook over low flame until the broccoli is thawed. Add the butter or margarine. Add all the remaining ingredients except the cheese and blend together. Sprinkle the cheese on top. Bake in a 300° F. oven for 1½ hours. Serves 2 to 4.

Cornflict

(*Conflict*, 1936)

A prizewinning baked corn dish.

INGREDIENTS:
  2 cups whole kernel canned
    corn, drained
  2 tablespoons salted butter
  2 tablespoons all-purpose flour
1¼ cups milk
  1 tablespoon sugar
  2 large eggs

EQUIPMENT:
Saucepan
Small bowl
Small casserole dish

Melt the butter in the saucepan; stir in the flour and milk, stirring constantly until thick. Remove from heat. Beat the eggs well and add with all remaining ingredients to the milk mixture. Pour into a greased casserole dish and bake at 350° F. for 25 minutes. Serves 4 to 6.

Tycoon

Cast: John Wayne, Laraine Day, Sir Cedric Hardwicke,
Judith Anderson, James Gleason, Anthony Quinn
Director: Richard Wallace
Released by RKO Pictures (1947)

The best assessment of this misguided clinker came from critic James Agee, whose entire review consisted of: "In this movie, several tons of dynamite are set off—none of it under the right people."

We find it difficult to improve upon this succinct evaluation!

Tycorn

This is one zesty veggie.

INGREDIENTS:
- 2 10-ounce packages frozen corn
- 1 medium onion
- ½ cup thinly sliced celery
- 1 garlic clove
- 2 tablespoons salted butter
- 1 2-ounce jar diced pimento
- ½ teaspoon salt
- ¼ teaspoon dried basil leaves

EQUIPMENT:
3-quart saucepan with lid
Cutting board

Rinse the corn under running water to separate; drain. Chop the onion, slice the celery thin, and chop the garlic fine. Stir the onion, celery, and garlic in with the corn and cook in butter in the saucepan over medium heat, about 10 minutes or until the onion is tender. Stir in the remaining ingredients, reduce heat, and cover. Cook 5 minutes longer, or until corn is tender. Makes 6 to 8 servings.

Asparagus End

(*Adventure's End,* 1937)

They'll dive right in to this tasty take on asparagus.

INGREDIENTS:
6–10 *fresh asparagus spears*
  ½ *cup butter*
    Dash cayenne
    Dash paprika
    Pinch ground rosemary
    Pinch ground thyme
  1 *lemon*

EQUIPMENT:
Medium pot
Small bowl
Medium bowl

Steam the asparagus spears for 10 minutes, or until tender. Cream together the butter, cayenne, paprika, rosemary, and thyme. Blend in the juice from the lemon. Serve on drained hot asparagus. Serves 2 to 4.

A Man Beet-rayed

(*A Man Betrayed,* 1941—also called *Wheel of Fortune*)

If you're eating this before heading out to Club Inferno, make sure you keep the beet juice off your suit. It stains, you know.

INGREDIENTS:
12 *small fresh beets*
½ *cup sugar*
½ *tablespoon corn starch*
¼ *cup water*

¼ *cup white vinegar*
2 *tablespoons salted butter*

EQUIPMENT:
Medium to large pot

Mix the sugar and starch in the pot. Add the vinegar and water. Boil for 5 minutes. Add the beets to the heated sauce and let stand for 30 minutes. Just before serving, bring to a boil and add butter. Serves 4.

The Green Berets

Cast: John Wayne, David Janssen, Jim Hutton, Aldo Ray,
   Raymond St. Jacques
Directors: John Wayne and Ray Kellogg
Released by Warner Bros. (1968)

With the exception of *The Alamo* (1960), *The Green Berets* is probably Duke Wayne's most personal film in terms of relating his political philosophy. Wayne was appalled at the antiwar protests of the late 1960s and felt such sentiments were playing into the hands of Communist propagandists. Against all conventional wisdom, Wayne announced he would provide a major film which would support the U.S. government policy and our troops in the field. When Warner Bros. somewhat reluctantly agreed to finance the controversial movie, Wayne signed on as both star and director, despite the fact that the dual responsibility on *The Alamo* proved to be a nerve-racking experience.

Wayne shot *The Green Berets*—loosely based on Robin Moore's bestseller—in Georgia, which made a surprisingly suitable substitute for Southeast Asia. The Duke proved adept at handling the elaborate action sequences (along with Ray Kellogg). The characters and dialogue, however, were recycled from B World War II movies. Politically, the film was anything but subtle, with a vault of heavy-handed cliches used to justify U.S. policies.

Predictably, Duke's film was savaged by critics upon its release. Most found it deplorable that Wayne could make a movie so blatantly right wing. (The same critics, however, were somewhat less verbal in criticizing the barrage of empty-headed hippie-oriented films in release at the same time.)

Despite these controversies, the Duke had the satisfaction of appealing to the "Silent Majority." *The Green Berets* was a major moneymaker and became one of the top grossing films of the year.

Did You Know . . . ?

★ Vera Miles filmed a sequence as the Duke's wife. The scene was ultimately cut from the movie.

The Green Beanrets

Even Vietnam veterans need to eat their greens!

INGREDIENTS:
- 2 16-ounce cans French-cut green beans
- 1 10¾-ounce can condensed cream of mushroom soup
- ½ cup milk
- ¼ cup shredded Cheddar cheese
- 1 16-ounce can french fried onions
- 1 tablespoon salted butter or margarine
  Salt and pepper to taste

EQUIPMENT:
2½-quart baking dish
Medium bowl

Drain the water from beans and place them in the baking dish. In the bowl, mix the soup and milk, then pour the blend over the beans. Add the cheese, salt, pepper, and sprinkle fried onions on top. Place the butter in the middle, on top. Bake in a 350° F. oven for 30 minutes. Serves 6 to 8.

Reonion in France

(Reunion in France, 1942)

Michele served Talbot these french fried onion rings the night they fell in love. You may even fall in love with them, too.

INGREDIENTS:
- 1 *cup all-purpose flour*
- ½ *teaspoon salt*
- ½ *cup milk*
- 2 *tablespoons vegetable oil*
- 1 *large egg white*
- 6 *tablespoons water*
- 3 *large onions*
- *Canola oil*

EQUIPMENT:
Sifter
Medium bowl
Medium pot
Paper towel

Sift the flour together with salt. Add the milk, oil, and egg white, and beat until smooth. Add water and beat to make a thin batter. Peel and slice the onions into ¼-inch slices. Separate the rings of the onions. Dip the rings in the batter and fry them in hot cooking oil until golden brown, about 5 minutes on high flame, a few at a time. Drain them on paper towels and serve hot. Serves 2 to 4.

Three Fries West

(Three Faces West, 1940)

Three cheers for these hearty french fries.

INGREDIENTS:
- 4 medium russet potatoes
- 1 tablespoon vegetable oil
- ¼ teaspoon freshly ground black pepper
- ⅛ teaspoon salt
- 2 garlic cloves

EQUIPMENT:
- 2 large bowls
- Colander
- Paper towels
- Nonstick baking sheet

Cut the potatoes into large wedges. Mince the garlic and set aside. Place the potatoes in the bowl and add cold water to cover. Let stand for 15 minutes. Drain the potatoes in the colander, then dry thoroughly by pressing with paper towels. Place the potatoes in a clean bowl. Sprinkle with oil, pepper, and salt, and toss thoroughly to combine all ingredients. Arrange the potatoes on a single layer on a baking sheet, and bake in a 425° F. oven for 20 minutes. Turn the potatoes over, sprinkle with garlic, and bake until golden, about 20 minutes. (You may want to turn the baking sheet around after 10 minutes to promote even browning.) Serves 2 to 4.

El Dorado

Cast: John Wayne, Robert Mitchum, James Caan, Charlene Holt,
   Michele Carey, Arthur Hunnicut
Director: Howard Hawks
Released by Paramount Pictures (1967)

By 1966, the great director Howard Hawks had been relegated to making B movies. He desperately wanted to prove he still had the ability to direct major films. Duke Wayne, who had made *Red River* (1948), *Rio Bravo* (1959), and *Hatari!* (1962) with Hawks rode to the rescue by agreeing to star in *El Dorado,* a property that Hawks was trying to bring to the screen. Wayne would costar for the first and only time with Robert Mitchum in the fairly lighthearted western that bore more than a passing resemblance to *Rio Bravo.* Wayne is a gunman who rallies drunken sheriff Mitchum to defend some helpless ranchers against—what else?—an evil land baron. (Are there any other kind of land barons?)

The film was hardly groundbreaking, but critics liked it and it proved to be a major box office hit. It also enabled the old pros in the cast to work with Hawks, who seemed reinvigorated by the project. The movie is notable for presenting James Caan in one of his earliest—and most memorable—screen appearances as a courageous but nearsighted gunman.

There is a sentimental air about *El Dorado,* as though Wayne and Hawks realized they were in the twilight of their years and that their opportunities to work together were drawing to a close. As mentioned, the two would reunite on Hawks's last major film, *Rio Lobo,* but it would be the weakest of their collaborations.

Did You Know . . . ?

★ Much of *El Dorado* was filmed on the legendary western movie set in Old Tuscon, Arizona. During the production, town officials honored Wayne by naming a street John Wayne Drive. Duke had previously shot other westerns, including *Rio Bravo,* there.

El Potato

This twice-baked potatoes recipe was a favorite at the Broken Heart Saloon. Thanks to "Buckskin" Judy Hamilton for this recipe.

INGREDIENTS:
 4 *large baking potatoes*
 ½ *stick salted butter*
1½ *cups sharp Cheddar cheese,*
   shredded
 ½ *teaspoon celery salt*
 1 *teaspoon paprika*

¼ *cup parsley flakes*
 3 *tablespoons milk*

EQUIPMENT:
Large baking tray
Small saucepan
Mixing bowl

Poke each potato several times with a fork and fully bake them, for 45 minutes in a 425° F. oven on a baking tray. Remove the potatoes from the oven, cut each one in half, and allow to slightly cool.

Melt the butter in the saucepan and set aside. In the mixing bowl, combine 1 cup of the shredded cheese, celery salt, and half of the parsley flakes. Add the butter. Scoop out the warm potatoes onto the butter and cheese mixture (save those skins!). Add milk, and stir well. Spoon the potato mixture back into the potato skin shells, and place them back on the baking tray. Sprinkle with the remaining cheese, parsley, and paprika. Bake uncovered in a 350° F. oven for 10 to 15 minutes. Serves 4 to 6.

Santa Fe Stampeas

(*Santa Fe Stampede,* 1938)

You'll strike gold, too, when these delicious peas hit your spoon.

INGREDIENTS:
- 2 *tablespoons olive oil*
- 1 *garlic clove*
- 1 *medium white onion*
- 2 *tablespoons minced fresh parsley*

2½ *cups fresh peas*
¼ *cup water*
Salt and pepper to taste

EQUIPMENT:
Large saucepan

Mince the garlic and slice the onion. Heat the olive oil in a pan over medium-high heat. Saute the garlic, onion, and parsley until browned. Add the peas and season with salt and pepper. Cook for about 1 minute over medium flame, stirring constantly. Add water, cover the pan, and simmer for 10 minutes. Makes 6 servings.

The Oregano Trail

(*The Oregon Trail,* 1936)

What elevates this eggplant recipe above the norm is the plentiful addition of the herb, oregano. Thanks for this recipe to Dolores Fantarella.

INGREDIENTS:
1 *large eggplant*
  All-purpose flour
2 *large eggs*
  Plain bread crumbs
  Olive oil
2 *medium tomatoes*
  Grated Romano cheese
  Dried oregano

EQUIPMENT:
3 small bowls
Medium frying pan
Casserole dish
Paper towels

Peel the eggplant and slice into thin round slices. Beat the eggs and sprinkle them with salt and pepper. Coat each eggplant piece with flour, then dip into the eggs, then in the bread crumbs. Fry each piece in olive oil over medium flame until both sides are browned. Drain on paper towels.

Form layers in a glass Pyrex dish of eggplant, sliced tomato, and grated cheese. Sprinkle with oregano. Layer until the dish is filled. Bake in a 350° F. oven for 15 to 20 minutes. Serve as a side dish or on a sandwich. Serves 4 to 6.

The Searchers

Cast: John Wayne, Jeffrey Hunter, Vera Miles, Ward Bond,
Natalie Wood, John Qualen, Olive Carey, Harry Carey, Jr.,
Ken Curtis
Director: John Ford
Released by Warner Bros. (1956)

For many critics and film historians, this 1956 western represents the pinnacle of the careers of John Wayne and John Ford. Returning to their beloved Monument Valley, the duo knew that this story had the making of something special. For Duke, the role of Ethan Edwards was the type of part that might come along but once in a lifetime. Edwards, a mysterious, ill-tempered drifter, returns to his brother's ranch presumably to finally settle down, though there are indications that he and his sister-in-law are secretly in love. The fragile relationship with the family is shattered when Indians raid the ranch, kill his brother and sister-in-law, and kidnap their two girls (one of whom is later murdered). Obsessed with revenge, Edwards embarks on a mission to track down the culprits, a journey which takes years. When he finally encounters his niece, their reunion provides one of the great sequences in film history.

Everyone was at their artistic peak in *The Searchers,* especially Ford, who reveled in rallying his stock company for one of his most ambitious films. As for the Duke, the role of Ethan Edwards led to the finest reviews of his career. Wayne would never again play a man so complex and morally ambiguous. His performance has been justifiably described as "towering."

Although *The Searchers* was a critical and box office hit at the time of its release, it was not until many years later that a new generation of filmmakers ensured that it received the hallowed status it so richly deserved. Martin Scorsese makes a point of watching the movie at least twice a year, and Steven Spielberg has labeled it the greatest motion picture ever made.

Did You Know . . . ?

★ "That'll be the day," Wayne's catch-phrase in the film, inspired singer Buddy Holly to write and perform the rock 'n' roll classic of the same name.

The Searchers' Beans

Here's a hearty baked-bean dish that Ethan Edwards might have enjoyed while tracking down the bloodthirsty Chief Scar. Hopefully, there are only *friendly* Indians in your territory!

INGREDIENTS:
- 2 16-ounce cans pork and beans
- ¾ cup dark brown sugar
- 2 teaspoons dry mustard
- 5 slices bacon
- ½ cup ketchup
- 1 teaspoon salt
- 1 teaspoon pepper
- 3 tablespoons barbecue sauce (your favorite)

EQUIPMENT:
1½-quart casserole dish
Small frying pan

Fry the bacon in the pan, drain thoroughly, chop, and set aside. Partially drain the pork and beans. Pour half of the beans into the casserole dish. Combine the brown sugar and mustard, and sprinkle over the beans. Top with the rest of the beans, and add chopped bacon, ketchup, and barbecue sauce. Mix it all thoroughly. Sprinkle on salt and pepper. Bake uncovered in a 325° F. oven for 2 hours. Serves 4 to 6.

Enjoying some Mother MacCream.

TRAIL'S END
DESSERTS AND SNACKS

Big Jake...A legend of a man.
A man who fought his way through hell
to save a grandson he had never seen!

John Wayne · Richard Boone

"Big Jake"

A CINEMA CENTER FILMS PRESENTATION

co-starring Patrick Wayne · Christopher Mitchum
Bobby Vinton · Bruce Cabot · Glenn Corbett · John Doucette

and Maureen O'Hara as MARTHA

Written by HARRY JULIAN FINK and R. M. FINK Produced by MICHAEL WAYNE Directed by GEORGE SHERMAN Music by ELMER BERNSTEIN
TECHNICOLOR® PANAVISION® A BATJAC PRODUCTION A NATIONAL GENERAL PICTURES RELEASE G

Big Jake

Cast: John Wayne, Richard Boone, Maureen O'Hara, Patrick Wayne,
Chris Mitchum, Bobby Vinton, Bruce Cabot, Harry Carey, Jr.,
Ethan Wayne
Director: George Sherman
Released by National General Films (1971)

*B*ig Jake offered Duke Wayne one of his last, precious opportunities to
work with an aging group of fellow actors and technicians. While he
would continue to make films over the next five years, *Big Jake*—in
many ways—represented the end of the traditional Duke Wayne western.
The movie reunited him with Maureen O'Hara for the first time since
McLintock! in 1963 and allowed him to work one last time under the
direction of George Sherman, who had collaborated with Duke on B
westerns in the 1930s. Wayne also enjoyed costarring with old cronies
Richard Boone (*The Alamo*) and stock company regular Bruce Cabot,
who died shortly after the release of *Big Jake.* In addition, the Duke
made the project a family affair, giving ample screen time to sons Patrick
and Ethan.

The film presents the Duke as Big Jake McCandles, a gruff, arro-
gant man who returns to his estranged wife in order to rescue the grandson he has never seen from a band of ruthless kidnappers who are

demanding a million dollar ransom. The film is an enormously enjoyable romp which—although somewhat bloody by Wayne standards—never takes itself too seriously. The sequences between Wayne and O'Hara are very touching, and Richard Boone makes a very memorable antagonist for the Duke. *Big Jake* boasts some excellent action set pieces and imaginative direction by George Sherman.

The film—which was a considerable box office hit—remains a highlight of Wayne's later career.

Did You Know . . . ?

★ The original title for *Big Jake* was "The Million Dollar Kidnapping."

Big Cake

The only cake that could satisfy the big guy himself. Thanks to "Big" Betty Hamilton.

INGREDIENTS:

CAKE:
 2 *large eggs*
 1 *cup sugar*
 1 *teaspoon vanilla extract*
 1 *cup all-purpose flour*
 1 *teaspoon baking powder*
 ¼ *teaspoon salt*
 ⅓ *cup milk*
 1 *teaspoon salted butter*

ICING:
 6 *tablespoons melted, salted butter*
 8 *tablespoons dark brown sugar*
 3 *tablespoons milk*

EQUIPMENT:
Small pan
Large bowl
9-inch round, greased cake pans
Cake plate

Heat the milk and one teaspoon of butter in a small pan until the butter melts. Mix the cake ingredients in a large bowl, then add the butter mixture. Mix together well. Pour into the cake pans and bake for 20 minutes in a 400° F. oven.

While the cake is baking, prepare the icing mixture. Remove the cake from the oven when done. Remove the cake from the pans and place the bottom layer on a serving plate. Pour one-third to one-half of the icing on the bottom layer while the cake is still warm. Place the next layer on top of bottom layer, and pour on the remaining icing, spreading it around until the entire cake is covered. Serves 4 to 6.

Heath Arizona Skies

('Neath Arizona Skies, 1934)

Heath bars—those classic Old West treats—are the main ingredient of this yummy dessert.

INGREDIENTS:
- 1 *box devil's food cake mix*
- 1 *large package (6 ounces) chocolate pudding mix*
- 1 *large container Cool Whip (16 ounce)*
- 6 *Heath bars*

EQUIPMENT:
Large trifle bowl
Small bowl
8 parfait glasses

Prepare the cake mix as directed, and let cool. Make the pudding and refrigerate.

Break the Heath bars into pieces and set aside. In a large trifle bowl, break up the cooled cake and form layers: a layer of crumbled cake, a layer of pudding, a layer of broken candy, a layer of Cool Whip, until finished. Sprinkle the top of the Cool Whip with the broken Heath bars, then refrigerate. Serves 4 to 6.

The Three Mousseketeers

(*The Three Musketeers,* released as *Desert Command,* 1933)

Three different flavors of mousse. Mix a batch of your favorite.

CHOCOLATE

INGREDIENTS:
- 1 12- to 16-ounce bar
  semisweet chocolate
- 8 large eggs
- ½ pint heavy cream
- ½ cup sugar
- 1 tablespoon brandy
- 2 dozen ladyfingers

EQUIPMENT:
- 2 medium bowls
- Double boiler
- Cake plate

Separate the eggs and set aside. Melt the chocolate in the double boiler over low flame and cool slightly. Beat the egg yolks and add to the chocolate. Add the cream.

Make a meringue of beaten egg whites, then add sugar gradually. Split the ladyfingers and sprinkle with brandy. Arrange the ladyfingers on the cake plate.

Combine the chocolate mixture with the meringue, then cover the ladyfingers with the mixture. Continue to create layers of the ingredients until a cake is formed. Chill well before serving. Makes 10 to 12 servings.

STRAWBERRY

INGREDIENTS:

2 packages strawberry Jello
   (3 ounces each)
2 cups boiling water
1 20-ounce package frozen
   strawberries
1 8-ounce tub Cool Whip

EQUIPMENT:

Small bowl
Medium bowl
Serving bowl

Dissolve the gelatin in boiling water. Add frozen berries, stirring until the fruit separates and the mixture thickens. Fold in the dessert topping. Pour the mixture in the serving dish and chill for 2 hours before serving. Makes 8 to 10 servings.

An equal amount of Cool Whip or other dessert topping can be substituted for the dessert topping mix.

COCONUT

INGREDIENTS:

1½ packages (3 ounces)
   unflavored gelatin
¼ cup cold water
1½ cups scalded milk
½ cup sugar
½ cup shredded coconut
½ teaspoon almond extract
1 cup heavy cream
1 pint strawberries

EQUIPMENT:

Medium bowl
Pie pan
Large bowl
Ring mold

Dissolve the gelatin in cold water in a medium bowl, and set the bowl in a pan of hot water. Combine the milk and sugar and stir until dissolved. Add the gelatin mixture, coconut, and almond. Pour into the bowl and refrigerate until partially set. Whip the cream and fold into the mixture. Pour into a ring mold and refrigerate until firm. Unmold, and fill the center with strawberries. Serves 4.

Lady Takes a Cheesecake

(*Lady Takes a Chance,* 1943)

Hopefully she saved some cake for the rest of us.

INGREDIENTS:
- 2 *tablespoons corn starch*
- 6 *large eggs*
- 4 *8-ounce packages cream cheese*
- 2 *cups sugar*
- 2 *tablespoons vanilla extract*

1 *pint sour cream*
  Cinnamon (ground)

EQUIPMENT:
Medium bowl
Small bowl
9-inch pie or baking pan

Beat the eggs, sugar, and corn starch until creamy. Soften the cream cheese (let it sit at room temperature for a half hour) and whip until smooth. Add other ingredients to the egg mixture, with the vanilla being last. Beat again while folding in the sour cream. Pour the mixture into the greased and floured pan. Sprinkle cinnamon on top. Bake at 350° F., until slightly browned (about 4 to 6 minutes), and then let stand in the oven for 10 minutes with the door open. Serves 2 to 4.

Texas Terrors

(*Texas Terror,* 1935)

Texas-size brownies that the prospectors just can't stop eating.

INGREDIENTS:
2 *cups sugar*
4 *large eggs*
1⅓ *cups vegetable oil*
6 *tablespoons cocoa*
2 *teaspoons vanilla extract*
2 *cups flour*
1 *teaspoon salt*
1 *teaspoon baking powder*

ICING:
1 *stick softened salted butter*
2 *cups confectioners' sugar*
2 *teaspoons vanilla extract*
4 *tablespoons cocoa*
¼ *cup milk*

EQUIPMENT:
2 *large mixing bowls*
Sifter
12 × 9-inch baking pan

Beat the eggs and combine with the sugar. Add the oil, cocoa, and vanilla. Sift together the flour, salt, and baking powder, and then sift into the batter, stirring occasionally. Put into a greased pan. Bake for 30 minutes in a 300° F. oven. While cooking, prepare the icing: Blend all the ingredients, along with enough milk to make the icing to the desired consistency (about ¼ cup). Allow the cooked brownies to cool slightly, then cover them with the icing.

For an exceptional taste treat, add your favorite unsalted chopped nuts to the brownie batter before baking. (Walnuts? How about peanuts or macadamias?) Serves 4 to 6.

Stagecoach

Cast: John Wayne, Claire Trevor, Andy Devine, Thomas Mitchell,
John Carradine, George Bancroft, Louise Platt, Berton Churchill,
Tim Holt, Donald Meek
Director: John Ford
Released by United Artists (1939)

Until *Stagecoach,* the Hollywood western had generally been represented by low-budget B oaters in which the hero wore a ten-gallon white
hat and the villain dressed entirely in black. Then director John Ford
purchased the screen rights to the story "Stage to Lordsburg" and set
about revolutionizing the genre. Ford resisted studio attempts to cast
Gary Cooper as "the Ringo Kid," the dangerous, but somehow naïve
outlaw who helps guide a besieged stagecoach through hostile Indian
territory. Instead, he fought to cast Wayne in the pivotal role. The opportunity proved to be a mixed blessing for the Duke, at least initially. The
ill-tempered Ford berated Wayne constantly and humiliated the actor in
front of the cast and crew. Years later, he said his strategy was to make
the Duke angry so that his performance would have an edge to it. This
was small comfort to Wayne at the time, however.

Ford indeed succeeded in making a mature, innovative western
which was immediately proclaimed a masterpiece. With a talented cast
and the stunning beauty of Monument Valley as his backdrop, he created

one of the screen's greatest works. Duke learned to accept his mentor's gruff manner and formed a close personal friendship with Ford, whom he would nickname Pappy. The two men would eventually create a series of motion pictures which would span four decades and represent the American cinema at its best.

Did You Know . . . ?

★ In the early 1970s, the American Film Institute announced that every known 35mm print of *Stagecoach* was in various states of disintegration—the film was in danger of literally fading away. A mint-condition print was finally donated to the AFI by John Wayne—who discovered it in his garage!

Stagecookie

Simple, yet delicious, party cookies passed around by the stagecoach passengers. Thanks to Betty "Dallas" Hamilton for this recipe.

INGREDIENTS:
1 cup dark brown sugar, firmly
   packed
½ cup sugar
1 cup shortening
2 large eggs
1½ teaspoons vanilla extract

2 cups all-purpose flour
1 teaspoon baking soda
1 teaspoon salt

EQUIPMENT:
Large bowl
Cookie sheets

Cream together the shortening, sugars, and eggs, and then add the rest of the ingredients and mix until smooth. Place teaspoon-size drops of dough onto the cookie sheets. Bake for about 8 minutes at 375° F.—but don't let them get too brown! Yields about 2 dozen stagecookies.

The Pie and the Mighty

(*The High and the Mighty,* 1954)

A classic blueberry pie, served on Trans-Orient-Pacific Airlines.

INGREDIENTS:
   Baked 9-inch pie shell
¼ cup cold water
5 tablespoons all-purpose flour
4 cups fresh blueberries
1 cup sugar

½ cup water
Pinch salt

EQUIPMENT:
Small bowl
Large pot

Make a smooth paste of the water, flour, and salt. Boil 1 cup of the blueberries with sugar and ½ cup of water. Add the flour paste and stir until all thickens. Remove from the stove and cool.

  When cool, add the remaining berries and put the mixture into the pie shell. Refrigerate. When cold, add Cool Whip topping (optional).

Back to Pecan

(*Back to Bataan,* 1945)

They'll keep coming back to this pie, much like Colonel Madden and his men must go back to Bataan.

INGREDIENTS:
1 cup light corn syrup
1 cup granulated sugar
2 tablespoons salted butter,
  softened
3 large eggs
¼ teaspoon salt

1 cup pecans
1 9-inch unbaked pastry shell
  or pie crust

EQUIPMENT:
Medium bowl
9-inch pie tin

Slightly beat the eggs in the bowl. Add the corn syrup, butter, sugar, and salt, and mix thoroughly. Spoon into the pastry shell and cover with pecan halves. Bake in a 350° F. oven for 1 hour. (Poke with fork to test—if it comes out clean, it's done.)

The Longest Day

Cast: John Wayne, Richard Burton, Henry Fonda, Robert Mitchum,
Robert Ryan, Red Buttons, Sean Connery
Directors: Ken Annakin, Andrew Marton, Bernhard Wicki,
Darryl F. Zanuck
Released by Twentieth Century–Fox (1962)

Darryl F. Zanuck's massive reenactment of the D-Day invasion at Normandy has certainly earned its place among the cinema's greatest achievements. Armed with a huge budget of $10 million, Zanuck and an army of technical advisors created a breathtaking work that was unique among spectacles. Although the battle sequences are spectacular, the script never deviates from focusing on how the conflict affected individual soldiers on both sides.

Zanuck had succeeded in signing up a virtual "who's who" of major stars, each of whom agreed to appear for a mere $25,000. When Zanuck approached Duke Wayne, however, he received a rebuke. It seems the Duke was peeved about sarcastic comments Zanuck had made about *The Alamo* the year before. Ultimately, Wayne demanded—and received—the startling sum of $250,000 for four days work!

Wayne, playing Lt. Col. Benjamin Vandervoot, appears onscreen less than twelve minutes, but through excellent editing his presence dominates a good percentage of the film. This is still not a "John Wayne

 173

Vandervoot briefs the troops on how to assemble The Longest Parfait.

movie" in the traditional sense. Wayne is but one participant in a truly memorable homage to the kind of heroism and courage we may never see again. *The Longest Day* is a classic in every sense of the word.

Did You Know . . . ?

★ In addition to getting his extravagant salary, Wayne had also ensured that he would receive special billing so that he would stand apart from the other stars, who were listed alphabetically.

The Longest Parfait

A dessert enjoyed by the combined forces after their assault on Normandy. With thanks to "General" Judy Hamilton.

INGREDIENTS:
- 1 3-ounce box instant vanilla pudding
- 1 3-ounce box instant chocolate pudding
- 1½ cups granola cereal
- 1 can Reddi Wip cream
- Fresh fruit (optional)

EQUIPMENT:
- 8 parfait glasses

Make pudding according to directions on boxes.

Alternately fill the parfait glasses with a spoonful of vanilla pudding, covering with granola, then a spoonful of chocolate pudding until the glass is full. Top each glass with whipped cream. Chill for 1 hour. Serves 6 to 8.

For a tasty treat, add a layer of your favorite fresh fruit (strawberries, blueberries, peaches, etc.) as you pile up your parfait!

She Wore a Yellow Ribbon

Cast: John Wayne, Joanne Dru, John Agar, Ben Johnson,
  Harry Carey, Jr., Victor McLaglen, Mildred Natwick,
  George O'Brien
Director: John Ford
Released by RKO Radio Pictures (1949)

John Ford and his ever-expanding "stock company" of favorite actors returned to the magnificent location of Monument Valley for *She Wore a Yellow Ribbon,* by far the most sentimental of his "Cavalry Trilogy." With John Wayne's triumph in *Red River* (1948) fresh in Ford's mind, the director did not hesitate to cast the Duke in another role which would require him to age beyond his years. Duke plays Capt. Nathan Brittles, a hard-bitten, yet softhearted commander of an outpost in the heart of hostile Indian territory. Days away from an uneasy retirement, the career army officer is faced with last-minute obstacles, including an Indian uprising and a number of domestic crises in his personal life.

On many occasions, Duke has named the character of Brittles as his favorite role, and he received universal praise for his outstanding performance. Surprisingly, although he was nominated for an Oscar that year, it was not for his inspired work on *Ribbon,* but rather his more conventional role in *Sands of Iwo Jima.*

She Wore a Jell-O Ribbon

The whipped cream on top of this cake conceals a tasty surprise: a ribbon of Jell-O spreading throughout the dessert!

INGREDIENTS:
   White cake mix
1 *small (3-ounce) box*
   strawberry Jell-O
16 *ounces Cool Whip*

EQUIPMENT:
Large bowls for preparing cake
  and Jell-O
2 9-inch cake pans
Dinner plate

Prepare the cake according to directions on the box. Remove the cake from the pans, and stack the two halves on the plate on top of each other. Prepare the Jell-O according to directions, but do not let it set. Puncture holes in the top of the cake (try using a meat thermometer, and poke down as deep as you can). Pour the Jell-O into the holes. Top with Cool Whip and refrigerate overnight. Serves 4.

Angel Food Cake and the Badman

(*Angel and the Badman,* 1947)

Angel food cake with a hint of chocolate.

INGREDIENTS:
¾ *cup cake flour*
¼ *cup cocoa*
¼ *teaspoon salt*
1 *teaspoon cream of tartar*
2 *cups egg whites (from*
   approx. 14 to 16 large eggs)

1 *teaspoon vanilla extract*
1½ *cups sugar*

EQUIPMENT:
Sifter
2 medium bowls
1 standard size tube pan

Sift together the flour, cocoa, and salt. Add cream of tartar to the egg whites and beat them until they will hold peaks. Add the vanilla, then the sugar gradually, and fold this mixture into the flour mixture. Pour the batter into an ungreased tube pan and bake for 45 minutes at 350° F.

The Alamo

Cast: John Wayne, Richard Widmark, Laurence Harvey,
   Richard Boone, Frankie Avalon, Patrick Wayne, Linda Cristal,
   Chill Wills
Director: John Wayne
Released by United Artists (1960)

By far the proudest and most personal of his film projects, *The Alamo* represented the culmination of a life's dream for John Wayne. He had long wanted to bring the heroic story of the fight for Texas independence from Mexico to the screen. After twenty years of planning, he secured a then whopping $7.5 million budget from United Artists and private investors. The Duke was primarily concerned with producing and directing the massive epic, but the studio insisted he star as Davy Crockett as well. The triple duty proved so damaging to Duke's nerves that he began smoking up to 120 cigarettes a day! Wayne's cast was full of big names and the sets were magnificent—and costly. The film's budget ultimately soared to $12 million, with Wayne financing the overage himself by hocking everything he had.

Critics were lukewarm to the movie, but it did garner numerous Oscar nominations. An insulting ad campaign to solicit Academy votes backfired, however, when Wayne's co-star Chill Wills (who was nominated for Supporting Actor) implied that a vote against *The Alamo* was a vote against America. The result: only one win in a minor category (Sound). Over the years, however, the movie has built up a large and enthusiastic following, and Wayne lived to see the film gain a good deal of respect among cinema buffs. Ironically, though it would eventually turn a large profit, Duke had been forced to sell his percentage in the movie and never made a dime from it. Still, as an effort from a first-time director, *The Alamo* emerges as a major achievement.

Did You Know . . . ?

★ The fascinating story behind the film inspired an entire book, *John Wayne's "The Alamo,"* by Chris Andersen and Don Clark (Citadel Press).

The Alamode

The real reason for the attack on the fort: Santa Anna's men heard Crockett and his men were enjoying this ice cream cake behind its walls.

INGREDIENTS:
 3 *large eggs*
 ¼ *teaspoon salt*
 ¼ *cup sugar*
 1 *teaspoon vanilla extract*
 ¾ *cup pancake mix*
  Confectioners' sugar
  (approximately 1 teaspoon)
  Vanilla ice cream (1 quart)
  Chocolate syrup (approx. ½ cup)

Nuts (walnuts or pecans)
Chocolate ice cream
(1 quart)
Whipped cream

EQUIPMENT:
Mixing bowl
10 × 15-inch shallow pan
Wax paper
Towel

Combine the eggs and salt, and beat well. Gradually beat in the sugar, but only about 1 tablespoon at a time; add vanilla. Lightly fold in the pancake mix, blending to a smooth batter. Spread evenly in a pan lined with greased and floured wax paper. Bake at 400° F. for 7 to 8 minutes.

Turn the cake out on a towel sprinkled generously with confectioners' sugar. Remove the paper, and cut the cake into three equal pieces. Place even slices of vanilla ice cream on one piece of cake, and drizzle with chocolate syrup and nuts. Top with a second piece of cake. Cover with chocolate ice cream, then more syrup and nuts. Top with the third piece of cake, and cover with whipped cream. Freeze. Makes 8 servings.

North to Baked Alaska

(North to Alaska, 1960)

You'll strike it rich, too, when you indulge in this delicious dessert.

INGREDIENTS:
- *1 angel food cake or sponge cake*
- *4 egg whites*
- *⅛ teaspoon cream of tartar*
- *½ cup sugar*
- *1 quart vanilla ice cream*
- *1 small box (approx. 8 ounces) frozen blueberries*

EQUIPMENT:
Small cutting board
Medium bowl

Soak a small cutting board in water for 30 minutes; dry. Place the cake on the board. Beat the egg whites and cream of tartar until stiff. Gradually beat in the sugar; continue beating until very stiff. Scoop out the center of cake, enough so that the ice cream will fit into the hole. Pack the ice cream into the center of the cake. Pour the blueberries onto the ice cream. Cover with the egg white mixture, being sure to completely cover the cake and ice cream so that it will be "sealed." Bake about 5 minutes at 450° F. or until lightly browned. Serve at once. Makes 6 to 8 servings.

Circus World

Cast: John Wayne, Rita Hayworth, Lloyd Nolan, Richard Conte,
   John Smith
Director: Henry Hathaway
Released by Paramount Pictures (1964)

Overlong and overblown, *Circus World* was a misguided, big-budget love story and adventure, with Duke Wayne as the unlucky owner of a tragedy-plagued circus traveling through Europe. The film was to be directed by the great Frank Capra, but the legendary filmmaker ran afoul of the Duke when he refused the script, which was rewritten by Wayne's longtime (and long-winded) collaborator James Edward Grant. Capra resigned and was replaced by Henry Hathaway, who would eventually make such excellent films as *The Sons of Katie Elder* (1965) and *True Grit* (1969) with the Duke. Alas, *Circus World* was not to be in that league. The script was talky and predictable, and the presence of a few large-scale action sequences and good location scenery was scant compensation. The film's one true highlight—the devastating fire which engulfs the big top—is too little, too late. The rest of *Circus World* is a three-ring bore.

Did You Know . . . ?

★ The climactic fire sequence proved to be equally dangerous off-screen, when the flames quickly spread out of control. Wayne, who was preoccupied with performing some stunts in the midst of the action, was nearly killed when the fleeing cast and crew neglected to inform him of the real danger!

Circus World Popcorn Treats

A new twist on the circus favorite.

INGREDIENTS:
 5 quarts hot popcorn
 ⅔ cup molasses
1½ cups sugar
 ¼ teaspoon salt
 1 teaspoon white vinegar
 3 tablespoons butter

EQUIPMENT:
Large saucepan
Large bowl

Combine the molasses, sugar, salt, and vinegar in the saucepan. Heat the mixture to a hard boil. Remove from the heat, add butter, and stir until fully melted. Pour over the popcorn. Grease your hands and roll the popcorn into small balls. Makes about 18 balls.

Rio Jell-O

(*Rio Lobo,* 1971)

A favorite dessert of Colonel McNally and his soldiers.

INGREDIENTS:
 2 3-ounce packages raspberry
    Jell-O
 2 cups boiling water
 1 20-ounce can crushed
    pineapple, undrained

 1 cup blueberries or
    strawberries
    Chopped walnuts (about 2–4
    ounces)

TOPPING:
8 ounces soft cream cheese
8 ounces sour cream
½ cup sugar
1 teaspoon vanilla

EQUIPMENT:
Large bowl
9 × 13-inch pan

Mix the Jell-O and water until dissolved. Add the pineapple and berries. Pour into the pan and chill until congealed.

Cream together the topping ingredients and spread over the Jell-O. Sprinkle with chopped walnuts. Refrigerate. Serves 2 to 4.

Dark Chocolate Command

(*Dark Command,* 1940)

A candy-bar cake that will take command of your dessert table.

INGREDIENTS:
2 sticks salted butter
2 cups sugar
4 large eggs
8 chocolate bars (approx. 2 ounces each; dark chocolate works best)
2 teaspoons vanilla extract
2½ cups cake flour
¼ teaspoon salt
¼ teaspoon baking soda
1 cup buttermilk

EQUIPMENT:
Small pan
Small bowl
Large bowl
Standard tube or loaf pan

Melt the candy bars in a small pan over low heat and set aside. Cream together the butter and sugar. Add the eggs one at a time, then all remaining ingredients, and mix well. Pour the mixture into the pan and bake at 300° F. for 1½ hours. Add your favorite frosting, or enjoy unfrosted. Makes 12 servings.

Lady for a Night

Cast: Joan Blondell, John Wayne, Ray Middleton
Director: Leigh Jason
Released by Republic Pictures (1942)

Hopelessly corny and unbelievably offensive in terms of racial stereotypes, *Lady for a Night* is one of the few Duke Wayne movies that even purists can be advised to skip. The film is so bad it makes *Big Jim McLain* look like *King Lear.*

Ladyfinger for a Night

All of Memphis society loved these ladyfingers.

INGREDIENTS:

¾ pound salted butter
4 cups sifted all-purpose flour
½ teaspoon baking powder
2 tablespoons sugar
1 large egg yolk

4 tablespoons cold water
1 pint raspberry jam
1 tablespoon salted butter
1 tablespoon milk
½ cup confectioners' sugar
Vanilla extract to taste

EQUIPMENT:

Large bowl	*Wax paper*
Medium bowl	*Baking sheet*
Small bowl	*Blender*

Rub ¾ pound of butter into the flour, baking powder, and sugar. Beat the egg yolk in water and add to the flour mixture. Mix to a stiff paste and divide into three equal parts. Roll one part very thick onto the wax paper. Prick all over with a fork, then turn over on the cookie sheet. Spread with raspberry jam.

Repeat with the other 2 parts in layers approximately 8 × 12 inches. Bake for 30 minutes at 350° F. Cut into fingers, about 1 × 3 inches.

Blend the remaining butter and milk, and blend in confectioners' sugar until the mixture comes to spreading consistency. Flavor with vanilla. Spread on cookies. Makes 40 cookies.

Butter Face

(*Baby Face,* 1933)

This butter cake is sure to put a smile on your baby's face. Thanks to "Grandma" Sophie Thumann.

INGREDIENTS:

CAKE:
- ½ *pound salted butter*
- 1 *cup sugar*
- 2 *large eggs*
- 2 *cups flour*
- 2 *teaspoons baking powder*
- ¾ *cup milk*
- 1 *teaspoon vanilla extract*

TOPPING:
- ½ *cup sugar*
- ¼ *pound salted butter*
- 1 *teaspoon ground cinnamon*

EQUIPMENT:

Mixer

Small pan

Small bowl

Large bowl

9 × 13-inch rectangular cake
   pan

Melt the butter in a small pan. Mix all the cake ingredients in the large bowl. Add ½ pound of butter. Mix thoroughly until smooth. Pour into the baking pan. Bake the cake in a 400° F. oven for 25 minutes.

    Melt the remaining butter for the topping in a small pan, and add in the small bowl, to the rest of the ingredients for the topping. Remove the cake from the oven. Spread the topping evenly over the cake and cook for 5 more minutes. Serves 6 to 8.

The Man Who Shot Liberty Valance

Cast: James Stewart, John Wayne, Vera Miles, Lee Marvin,
 Edmond O'Brien, Andy Devine, Woody Strode, John Carradine
Director: John Ford
Released by Paramount Pictures (1962)

Although the Duke would team once more with John Ford for the featherweight comedy *Donovan's Reef* (1963), *Liberty Valance* represents—for all intents and purposes—the last hurrah for their collaborative efforts. One of the most debated of all westerns, *Liberty Valance* is unique among Ford's films. It replaces his trademark sweeping landscapes with the claustrophobic atmosphere of a black-and-white film which was shot almost completely on sound stages. Many feel that Ford was making a parallel to the end of the Wild West as well as his style of moviemaking. Indeed, this was the last real project to feature his fabled stock company, and the somber air of the film reflects the fact that everyone knew this was nearing the end of "Pappy" Ford's career.

At the time, Wayne griped that he played second fiddle to Jimmy Stewart in this cynical story about a dude who gains fame as the killer of a notorious gunman. While Stewart certainly has the meatier role (and has top billing), Wayne is the more interesting character: a tired, weary tough guy who realizes all too late that his day is over.

Wayne and Stewart give magnificent performances and are matched by a superb supporting cast. Lee Marvin is especially good as one of the screen's immortal villains.

Ford probably should have retired with this film, instead of the glorified home movie that was *Donovan's Reef,* and his final effort, the ill-fated *7 Women* (1966). *Liberty Valance* is a true classic and one of the highlights of the master director's career.

Did You Know . . . ?

★ Although singer Gene Pitney had a hit song with "The Man Who Shot Liberty Valance," the track does not appear in the film. (James Taylor covered the song years later.)

The Flan Who Shot Liberty Valance

The legend of the outlaw, Liberty Valance, continues with this delectable dessert.

INGREDIENTS:
- 3 *cups milk*
- 1 *cup light cream*
- 6–8 *tablespoons instant coffee*
- 2 *teaspoons dried, grated orange rind*
- 4 *large whole eggs*
- 1 *large egg, separated*
- ½ *cup sugar*
- 1 *teaspoon vanilla extract*
- 1 *teaspoon almond extract*
- ½ *teaspoon salt*
- 1 *teaspoon ground nutmeg*
- 1 *cup chopped Brazil nuts*
- 3 *tablespoons guava jelly*

EQUIPMENT:
Small saucepan
Fine strainer
Large mixing bowl
Small mixing bowl
6 custard cups
9 × 13-inch shallow baking pan

Scald the milk in the saucepan together with the light cream. Add instant coffee and orange rind, and stir well. Cool for 10 minutes.

Beat whole eggs along with the egg yolk and sugar. Add the coffee mixture, extracts, and salt; blend well. Strain through a fine strainer. Pour the mixture into six custard cups. Sprinkle each with nutmeg. Place the cups in a shallow baking pan; fill the pan with cold water up to ¾ inch from the top of the cups. Bake at 325° F. for 1 hour, or until a knife inserted in the center comes out clean. Let cool, then refrigerate.

Just before serving, remove each custard mixture from its cup with a small spatula; arrange upside down on a serving dish. Sprinkle with Brazil nuts. Beat the egg white until stiff; beat in guava jelly until stiff. Swirl over the nuts.

Westward Dough

(*Westward Ho,* 1935)

Roll out the refrigerated dough, bake, and in no time you'll be devouring these icebox cookies.

INGREDIENTS:
- 2 *cups sugar*
- 1 *cup ground nuts (walnuts or pecans; optional)*
- 1 *teaspoon salt*
- 2 *teaspoons baking powder*
- 3 *large eggs*
- 5 *cups flour*
- 1 *tablespoon vanilla extract*
- 1 *pound salted butter*

EQUIPMENT:
Small bowl
Large bowl
Rolling pin
Cookie cutters

Cream together the sugar and butter; add beaten eggs. Mix in the rest of the ingredients by hand. Place in a covered container and let stand overnight in the refrigerator. Roll the dough approximately ⅛ inch thick; cut with cookie cutters. Decorate with sprinkles (if desired). Bake in a 350° F. oven for 8 to 10 minutes. Makes about 5 dozen cookies.

Island in the Pie

(*Island in the Sky,* 1953)

Fresh strawberries truly are islands in these pies.

INGREDIENTS:
- 1 *10-ounce package frozen strawberries, thawed*
- 1 *cup sugar*
- 1 *tablespoon lemon juice extract*
- 3–4 *whole strawberries*
- 2 *large egg whites*

- ½ *pint whipping cream*
- 2 *8-inch baked pie shells*
  Cool Whip

EQUIPMENT:
2 pie pans
Blender
Bowl

Beat together the thawed strawberries, sugar, lemon juice, and egg whites for 20 minutes. Fold in the whipping cream, then spoon the mixture into the pie shells. Place in the freezer overnight.

When serving, put a few whole strawberries and Cool Whip on top as you serve straight from the freezer.

The Greatest Story Ever Told

Cast: John Wayne, Max Von Sydow, Charlton Heston, Sal Mineo,
   Donald Pleasance, David McCallum, Telly Savalas, Sidney Poitier
Director: George Stevens
Released by United Artists (1965)

Among the most reverent and intelligent films about the life of Christ, *The Greatest Story Ever Told* was an ambitious dream project for the great director George Stevens. Unfortunately for the studio, Stevens's big-budget movie was a bit *too* reverent for general audiences. This thinking-man's epic was in total contrast to such empty-headed spectacles as *The Ten Commandments* (1956). However, the latter is more fun to watch, even if for all the wrong reasons.

The Greatest Story boasts an excellent cast and production values, but the slow pace and talky script makes one occasionally wish for the "so-bad-they're-good" films of Cecil B. DeMille. In a misguided attempt to spice up audience interest, Stevens made the mistake of casting well-known actors in absurd cameo roles until the film's crucifixion sequence begins to look like the Santa Claus Parade in Hollywood, with big names popping up for seconds at a time. The most inexcusable casting is that of the Duke as a Roman centurion who prods Jesus along to his death, only to be redeemed by his courage and gallantry. The sight of Wayne in

"Truly, this Jell-O is the best, by God!"

full costume as a Roman soldier is only outdone by his one line of dialogue: "Truly, this man was the son 'a god!" Despite its good intentions and excellent performances from less glamorous cast members, Stevens's film failed at the box office, and the legendary director would retire from making motion pictures.

Did You Know . . . ?

★ After the film's initially weak performance at the box office, the studio cut the nearly three hour running time for general release engagements. The restored, original length film is now available on videocassette.

The Greatest Jell-O Ever Mold

A unique dessert, made up of three delicious layers—almost as memorable as the sight of the Duke in sandals!

INGREDIENTS:
- 1 *3-ounce package cherry Jell-O*
- ⅔ *cup milk*
- 16 *marshmallows*
- 1 *8-ounce package cream cheese*
- 1 *3-ounce package lemon Jell-O*
- 1 *4-ounce can crushed pineapple*
- ⅔ *cup walnuts*
- 1 *cup Cool Whip*
- 1 *3-ounce package orange Jell-O*

EQUIPMENT:
Oblong cake pan or 2-quart glass casserole dish
Double boiler

Prepare cherry Jell-O according to directions and pour into an oblong cake pan. Chill to set.

For the second layer, heat the milk, marshmallows, and cheese over low heat in a double boiler until all is melted, then add lemon Jell-O. Let the mixture cool before adding pineapple, nuts, and Cool Whip. Stir together, then pour it over the first layer and chill.

The dessert is completed by preparing the orange Jell-O according to directions, then pouring it on top of the second layer. Let it set in the refrigerator.

You can substitute your favorite Jell-O flavors, but it's nice to have three different ones. Plus, the side view will look pretty cool if you prepared this in a glass casserole dish!

The Cowboys

Cast: John Wayne, Roscoe Lee Brown, Bruce Dern,
   Colleen Dewhurst, Slim Pickens, Lonnie Chapman
Director: Mark Rydell
Released by Warner Bros. (1972)

At an age at which most men are content to retire, Duke Wayne continued to break new ground in his profession with *The Cowboys,* his most unusual and ambitious role since *True Grit* (1969). Producer and director Mark Rydell made it clear that this would be a down-to-earth, realistic western, and that he wanted Wayne strictly as an actor, unencumbered by his own entourage and stock company. Recognizing the excellence of the script, Wayne agreed. He is cast as aging cattleman Wil Andersen, who is left in desperate need of cowhands to bring his herd to market after a gold strike causes his employees to desert him. He reluctantly hires a group of young schoolboys for the challenging and dangerous task. Accompanied by only one other adult—a cook named Mr. Nightlinger—he sets forth on his journey, knowing the odds are stacked against him.

Wayne is nothing less than brilliant as Wil Andersen, bringing a lifetime of experience and emotion to the role. To his credit, Wayne did not attempt to alter the script, which finds Wil shockingly murdered at the hands of rustlers. Duke is more than complemented by Roscoe Lee Brown (superb as Nightlinger), Bruce Dern (terrifying as the varmint who murders Wil), and a cast of professional and amateur young actors who give remarkable performances as Wil's hired cowhands. Rydell's direction is truly inspired, and the script is gloriously free of cliches and phony heroics.

While a hit at the box office, the film did not receive a single Oscar nomination. A true shame, since many of the aforementioned individuals were worthy of Academy consideration for this outstanding film.

Did You Know . . . ?

★ The film originally featured a meeting between Wil Andersen and a tribe of Indians. Although cut from the final version, the sequence appears on the videotape *John Wayne: Behind the Scenes With the Duke* (see the end of this book for ordering details).

Mr. Nightlinger's Old-Fashioned Apple Pie

Mr. Nightlinger's recipe called for "lard, cinnamon, a dab of butter, flour, salt, water to bind, sugar, and three slashes on the crust: one for steam, and two because your mama did it that way." We've taken a few liberties and filled in the blanks, but the results are just as delicious. Suggested by "Wild Bill" Wolfsthal.

INGREDIENTS:
- ¼ cup packed light brown sugar
- ¼ cup granulated sugar
- 1 tablespoon flour
- 1 teaspoon dried grated lemon peel
- ¼ teaspoon ground cinnamon
- ¼ teaspoon ground nutmeg
- 6 medium baking apples

1 cup raisins
1 unbaked, ready-made
  9-inch piecrust
  Honey (approx. 1 tablespoon)
  Cinnamon sugar (approx.
  1 teaspoon)

EQUIPMENT:
9-inch deep-dish pie plate
Pam cooking spray
Small bowl

Peel and core the apples and slice them thin. Spray the pie plate with the cooking spray. In a small bowl, mix well the sugars, flour, lemon peel, cinnamon, and nutmeg. Add the apples to the sugar mixture and stir until coated. Stir in the raisins and spoon the mixture into the prepared pie plate.

Place the pie crust on top of the filling and trim the edges, pressing against the edge of the pan. Using a sharp knife, be sure to cut three vents in the pie crust (as Nightlinger instructs). Sprinkle the top of pie with honey and cinnamon sugar.

Bake until the crust is golden, about 35 to 40 minutes in a 425° F. oven. Cool on a wire rack and serve warm.

Candy Rides Alone

(*Randy Rides Alone,* 1934)

Peanut clusters on which Randy snacked while rounding up the gang of outlaws.

INGREDIENTS:
 2 cups sugar
 1 cup evaporated milk
24 Kraft caramels
1½ cups chocolate chips

1 teaspoon vanilla extract
1 pound salted peanuts

EQUIPMENT:
Medium pot

Heat the sugar and milk; add the caramels. Boil for 4 minutes, after the caramels have melted. Remove from heat, add chocolate chips. Stir and add the vanilla and peanuts. Drop onto the wax paper in tea-spoonfuls, but work fast—the mixture hardens quickly. No baking necessary. Makes 5 to 6 dozen clusters.

Mother MacCream

(Mother Machree, 1928)

Enjoy this homemade peach ice cream which Mother served her son after they were reunited.

INGREDIENTS:
1 3-ounce package peach Jell-O
1 cup boiling water
½ teaspoon salt
1 10-ounce can peach slices
1 cup milk
1 cup heavy cream

EQUIPMENT:
Medium bowl
2 small bowls
8- or 9-inch square pan

Dice the peaches, whip the cream, and set both aside. Dissolve the gelatin in water, Stir in salt, the peaches, and their syrup. Chill until slightly thickened, to the consistency of unbeaten egg whites. Slowly stir in the milk, then fold in the whipped cream. Pour into the pan and freeze until firm. Makes 8 servings.

Range Fruit

(*Range Feud,* 1931)

A fruit salad made up of ingredients seldom found on the range, but it sounds good, anyway!

INGREDIENTS:

1 *20-ounce can pineapple chunks*

1 *16-ounce can sliced peaches*

1 *11-ounce can mandarin orange sections*

3 *medium bananas*

2 *apples*

1 *4-ounce box vanilla instant pudding*

1½ *cups milk*

½ *6-ounce can orange juice concentrate*

¾ *cup sour cream*

EQUIPMENT:

Large bowl

Extra large bowl

Drain the juice from all the canned fruit. Slice the apple into small wedges. Combine all the fruit, except the bananas, in the large bowl. Beat the pudding, milk, and juices in the larger bowl for 2 minutes. Fold in the sour cream, then fold in the fruit. Slice up the bananas and add them to the mixture. Serve cold. Makes 2 to 4 servings.

Cake of the Red Witch

(Wake of the Red Witch, 1948)

Fortunately, this carrot cake recipe didn't go down with the ship!

INGREDIENTS:
 2 *cups sugar*
1½ *cups vegetable oil*
 4 *large eggs*
 2 *cups self-rising flour*
 2 *teaspoons ground cinnamon*
 2 *teaspoons vanilla extract*
2½ *cups grated carrots*
 ½ *cup chopped walnuts*
 ¼ *cup salted butter*

 1 *8-ounce package cream*
   cheese
 1 *pound confectioners' sugar*
   Milk, if needed (⅛ cup)
   Shortening

EQUIPMENT:
3 cake pans
Small bowl
Large bowl

Beat the eggs in a small bowl and set aside. Grease the cake pans with the shortening and sprinkle with flour. In the large bowl, combine the sugar, oil, eggs, flour, cinnamon, 1 teaspoon of vanilla, the carrots, and nuts. Pour into the cake pans. Bake at 300° F. for 30 minutes. Let cool.

To make the icing, cream together the remaining ingredients. Add milk, if necessary, to make it more spreadable. Spread the icing onto the cake.

"That's what I'm trying to tell you: We're out of carrots!"

THE JOHN WAYNE FAN CLUBS

No true fan of John Wayne will want to pass up the opportunity to subscribe to these first-rate fan clubs dedicated to the legacy of the Duke.

The Big Trail is the long-running fan journal featuring in-depth analyses of Wayne's films; letters and observations from members throughout the world; the latest news and reviews of Wayne-related books, products, and videos; and exciting merchandise offerings. For subscription information, contact: Tim Lilley, editor; *The Big Trail,* 540 Stanton Avenue, Akron, Ohio, 44301

The John Wayne Film Society Newsletter: Proof that the Brits don't hold a grudge for all the chaos the Duke caused in London as Brannigan. This newsletter features reviews, bibliographies, biographies of Duke's coworkers, many rare photos, and information on products and film festivals. For information, write to: David Cutts, 129 Huthwaite Road, Sutton-in-Ashfield, Nottinghamshire, NG17 2GY England.

THE JOHN WAYNE BIRTHPLACE

The Duke's childhood home in Winterset, Iowa, is lovingly preserved by donations from fans. John Wayne admirers flock here to enjoy the modest house in which the legendary star was born. The birthplace is located at 216 South Second Street, Winterset, Iowa, 50273, and is open daily, 10:00 A.M. to 5:00 P.M., except Thanksgiving, Christmas, and New Year's Day. There is a modest admission fee, which allows guests to tour the facility and visit the Welcome Center and souvenir shop.

Fans are also encouraged to become either "Supporting Role" or "Starring Role" donors. In return for contributions, donors will receive various official John Wayne collectibles. For further information, call (515) 462-1044.

JOHN WAYNE COLLECTIBLE VIDEOS

Two exciting videos are now available from Spy Guise and Cara Entertainment featuring rare footage of the Duke.

John Wayne: Behind the Scenes With the Duke features ninety minutes of rarely seen, original production featurettes showing the Duke behind the scenes on classic movies such as *El Dorado, Chisum, In Harm's Way, McLintock!, The War Wagon, McQ, Brannigan,* and others. The video also features rare charity commercials with John Wayne.

The Duke and the General: The Lost Interviews With John Wayne and Jimmy Stewart features two of America's most beloved and legendary actors interviewed in this fascinating, rarely seen one-hour 1971 TV special, which aired only once. Both actors discuss their remarkable careers and their love for America. John Wayne is interviewed on the set of *The Cowboys* (and is shown in a sequence deleted from the final film), while Jimmy Stewart is seen shooting *Fool's Parade.* The video also features an original short about the making of *The Cowboys,* as well as trailers and collectibles from the movie.

Both tapes are recorded in the SP mode for maximum quality and are available for $23 each (postage included) from: Spy Guise, 263 Central Avenue, Jersey City, New Jersey 07307. Phone/fax: (732) 752-7257. (New Jersey residents please add 6 percent sales tax.) Credit cards accepted.

JOHN WAYNE FILMOGRAPHY

Mother Machree (1928)

Hangman's House (1928)

Salute (1929)

Words and Music (1929)

Men Without Women (1930)

Rough Romance (1930)

Cheer Up and Smile (1930)

The Big Trail (1930)

Girls Demand Excitement (1931)

Three Girls Lost (1931)

Men Are Like That (1931)

Range Feud (1931)

Maker of Men (1931)

Haunted Gold (1932)

Shadow of the Eagle (1932)

Hurricane Express (1932)

Texas Cyclone (1932)

Lady and Gent (1932)

Two-Fisted Law (1932)

Ride Him, Cowboy (1932)

The Big Stampede (1932)

The Telegraph Trail (1933)

Central Airport (1933)

His Private Secretary (1933)

Somewhere in Sonora (1933)

Life of Jimmy Dolan (1933)

The Three Musketeers (1933)

Baby Face (1933)

The Man From Monterey (1933)

Riders of Destiny (1933)

Sagebrush Trail (1933)

West of the Divide (1933)

Lucky Texan (1934)

Blue Steel (1934)

The Man From Utah (1934)

Randy Rides Alone (1934)

The Star Packer (1934)

The Trail Beyond (1934)

'Neath Arizona Skies (1934)

Lawless Frontier (1935)

Texas Terror (1935)

Rainbow Valley (1935)

Paradise Canyon (1935)

The Dawn Rider (1935)

Westward Ho (1935)

Desert Trail (1935)

New Frontier (1935)

Lawless Range (1935)

The Lawless Nineties (1936)
King of the Pecos (1936)
The Oregon Trail (1936)
Winds of the Wasteland (1936)
The Sea Spoilers (1936)
The Lonely Trail (1936)
Conflict (1936)
California Straight Ahead (1937)
I Cover the War (1937)
Idol of the Crowds (1937)
Adventure's End (1937)
Born to the West (1938)
Pals of the Saddle (1938)
Overland Stage Raiders (1938)
Santa Fe Stampede (1938)
Red River Range (1938)
Stagecoach (1939)
The Night Riders (1939)
Three Texas Steers (1939)
Wyoming Outlaw (1939)
New Frontier (1939)
Allegheny Uprising (1939)
Dark Command (1940)
Three Faces West (1940)
The Long Voyage Home (1940)
Seven Sinners (1940)
A Man Betrayed (1941)
Lady From Louisiana (1941)
The Shepherd of the Hills (1941)
Lady for a Night (1942)
Reap the Wild Wind (1942)
The Spoilers (1942)

In Old California (1942)
Flying Tigers (1942)
Reunion in France (1942)
Pittsburgh (1942)
Lady Takes a Chance (1943)
War of the Wildcats (1943)
The Fighting Seabees (1944)
Tall in the Saddle (1944)
Flame of the Barbary Coast (1945)
Back to Bataan (1945)
Dakota (1945)
They Were Expendable (1945)
Without Reservations (1946)
Angel and the Badman (1947)
Tycoon (1947)
Fort Apache (1948)
Red River (1948)
Three Godfathers (1948)
Wake of the Red Witch (1948)
She Wore a Yellow Ribbon (1949)
The Fighting Kentuckian (1949)
Sands of Iwo Jima (1949)
Rio Grande (1950)
Operation Pacific (1951)
Flying Leathernecks (1951)
The Quiet Man (1952)
Big Jim McLain (1952)
Trouble Along the Way (1953)
Island in the Sky (1953)
Hondo (1953)
The High and the Mighty (1954)
The Sea Chase (1955)